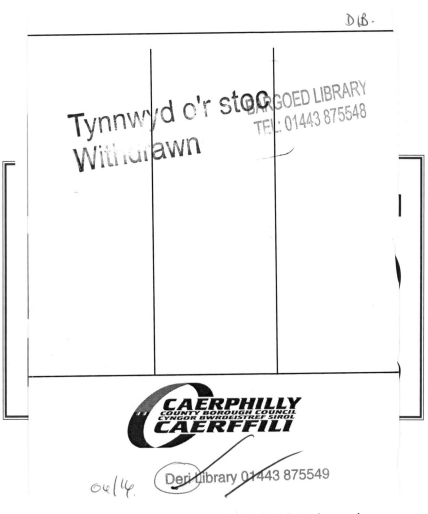

REAL FOOD PROJECTS

30 SKILLS. 46 RECIPES. FROM SCRATCH.

KATE WALSH

MURDOCH BOOKS

SYDNEY · LONDON

CONTENTS

INTRODUCTION

It's hard not to feel the change in the air. Backyards, allotments and balconies heaving with home-grown tomatoes and lettuce, people coming together to fill jars with seasonal pickles and jams, farmers' markets packed from dawn to dusk, and backyard chooks and beehives making a serious comeback. An ever-growing number of people want to improve their relationship with food and learn new skills in the kitchen.

Why are we heading back into the kitchen in droves?

People are waking up to the reality that what we eat and how we cook has a big hand in shaping our world. American poet and farmer Wendell Berry argues that 'eating is an agricultural act'. In other words, with every mouthful we take, we connect to the people who make our food and the type of food system we support. And it is this story, the story behind our food, which is making people increasingly uncomfortable.

We have found ourselves in the midst of a burgeoning industrialised food system that favours big business over small-scale, sustainable and resilient food producers. Our broken food system produces waste and causes obesity, is a major driver of climate change and is making us sick, yet still millions go hungry. Gone are the high streets full of bustling small businesses – the butchers, grocery stores, bakers and fruit shops. They've been replaced with large supermarket chains that dominate our consumer grocery market. They shape the kind of food we load in our trolleys and make it nearly impossible for smaller, family-owned businesses and local farms to survive. Taking seriously the responsibility of where to put our grocery dollars has never been more important.

Creative opportunities lie in making food chains better, not bigger. We need diverse, local food economies, where consumers can be guaranteed access to locally grown, ethical and affordable produce. This is no time for food-as-usual. To learn to cook might just be one of the most fundamental steps we can take to move away from our reliance on the industrialised food system and take an active part in building the food system we want.

But just as importantly, we are also rediscovering the pleasure of cooking and eating real food together. Over the past 40 years, we've been sold the idea that making food from scratch is too difficult, more expensive and too time-consuming. We responded by eating out more and relying on processed foods to feed our families. The irony is that we were meant to be happier without the drudgery of cooking when, in fact, it is the very act of buying the best seasonal produce we can, and cooking fresh, real food that brings us so much joy and pleasure.

Learning the magic of combining simple ingredients such as flour, water, yeast and salt to end up with a spectacular loaf of bread to share can be a revelatory act. To taste a peach at perfect ripeness and feel your tastebuds explode can be mind-blowing. Bringing people together to make the most of the tomato season builds community in a very special and authentic way. It is this feeling of connecting through real food that is bringing people back into the kitchen and back to the dining table.

We're also learning that eating foods containing a long list of numbers and odd-sounding ingredients makes us sick. The best way to make sure that you know what is in your food is to cook it yourself. I have found a simple joy in that sense of self-reliance, learning new skills and having the ability to do things in a better way. I want to pass that on to you and your family.

With this handbook by your side you will learn 30 food skills, step by step, which will put you on the path to learning how to cook a great deal of your food from scratch. You don't need a degree from a culinary college to make a wonderful jam, fiery mustard, great sausages or seriously good kim chi. Get started and learn what you love to cook.

The more often you make each project, the better you will understand the process and then you can jump off and be creative. The only way to learn how to cook is to make mistakes and make them often. Believe me, I've made my fair share. If your jam doesn't set, you have a great sauce for ice cream. If your sausages break, you'll have awesome-tasting mince for a spaghetti sauce. Mistakes or not, you'll learn something and next time it will be better.

I'm also a big believer in not using fancy, expensive kitchen equipment. I don't have the inclination to build a massive backyard smoker or make thousands of sausages. The projects in this book are for the home cook and the home kitchen so if you have a wooden spoon and a few bowls, you are well on your way. You will need a few bits of special equipment to make passata and sausages, but you won't be making these things every day and the tools can be shared between families.

I have given approximate yields for all the recipes, but be aware that they will change depending on the season. If it has been a good year for plums, they will be plump and full of juice and you'll get more jam. If it has been a tough year for peaches, the chutney yield will be less. This is part of the joy of cooking seasonally.

I want to help you change the way you eat and I hope this book will give you the skills, confidence and inspiration to get into the kitchen and have a crack at it. Good luck and let me know how you go!

CHAPTER ONE

GETTING STARTED

GRANOLA

Learning the simple art of making granola will wean you off supermarket breakfast cereals forever. And there is something so satisfying about the sweet smell of toasty granola fresh out of the oven. Making it is a regular ritual in my household, so there is always a huge jar of it in the pantry. This particular granola has lots of ginger, raisins and macadamia nuts, perfect for a cold winter's morning; you'll find other granola ideas on the following pages to enjoy throughout the seasons.

The instructions are really simple, so don't be daunted by the number of ingredients listed – they're all easy to find.

MAKES: 1 x 1 litre (32 oz) jar

INGREDIENTS

1 free-range egg white
1 tablespoon cold water
1 tablespoon light-tasting vegetable oil
90 g (3¼ oz/¼ cup) honey
1 teaspoon natural vanilla extract
40 g (1½ oz/¼ cup) pepitas (pumpkin seeds)
40 g (1½ oz/¼ cup) sunflower seeds
40 g (1½ oz/¼ cup) whole raw macadamia nuts
20 g (¾ oz/¼ cup) shredded coconut
1 teaspoon sea salt
1 teaspoon ground cinnamon
145 g (5 oz/1½ cups) rolled (porridge) oats (not the instant or quick-cooking variety)
100 g (3½ oz/½ cup) quinoa
85 g (3 oz/½ cup) raisins
110 g (3¾ oz/½ cup) unsugared crystallised ginger, cut into bite-sized pieces

EQUIPMENT

baking tray with small sides, or a lamington tin
baking paper
large bowl
small whisk or fork
wooden spoon
1 x 1 litre (32 oz) jar and lid

GRANOLA METHOD

(1) **Get your oven ready:** Preheat the oven to 160°C (315°F) and line a large baking tray with baking paper. It's best to use a tray that has sides, so the granola doesn't spill everywhere.

(2) »

Mix the wet ingredients: In a large bowl, whisk together the egg white and water until slightly foamy. Add the oil, honey and vanilla extract and give it a good stir.

«(3)

Add the dry ingredients: Add the seeds, nuts, coconut, salt, cinnamon, oats and quinoa. Stir vigorously with a wooden spoon, making sure all the ingredients are well coated.

Get ready to bake: Evenly spread the mixture over the lined baking tray, making sure the layer is no more than 1 cm (½ inch) thick, otherwise the granola won't crisp up nicely.

⑤ »

Bake: Toast in the oven for 30 minutes, or until golden brown, stirring every 10 minutes.

Cool: Allow to cool to room temperature, then break into small pieces, into a large clean bowl. Mix the raisins and ginger through.

Store: Transfer to a large clean jar or airtight container and store in the pantry. The granola will keep for up to 1 month.

HOW TO USE

- Top with home-made Yoghurt (page 95) and the leftover rhubarb from making the Rhubarb & quince cordial on page 33.
- Add melted butter and extra honey and press into a tin for granola bars.
- Bake without the nuts and serve as a healthy snack for kids' lunchboxes.
- Increase the amount of dried fruit and use as a healthy trail mix.
- Use the same process, omitting the grains and increasing the amounts and variety of nuts and seeds for a paleo granola.

Once you've made granola a few times, you can start to get creative. Change the amount of honey, and use different dried fruits and spices to make your ultimate breakfast. But remember – granola is not just for the morning. You can sprinkle it over poached fruit and serve with cream for dessert, or simply grab a handful whenever you walk past the jar. This is a much lighter summer version, with dried pineapple and coconut.

PINEAPPLE, ALMOND & COCONUT GRANOLA

MAKES: 1 x 1 litre (32 oz) jar

METHOD

Preheat the oven to 160°C (315°F) and line a large baking tray with baking paper. It's best to use a tray that has sides, so the granola doesn't spill out everywhere.

In a large bowl, whisk the egg white with the water until slightly foamy. Add the oil, honey and vanilla extract and give it a good stir.

Add the rest of the ingredients, except the dried pineapple and quinoa. Stir vigorously with a wooden spoon, making sure all the ingredients are well coated.

Evenly spread the mixture over the lined baking tray, making sure the layer is no more than 1 cm (½ inch) thick, otherwise the granola won't crisp up nicely. Toast in the oven for 30 minutes, or until golden brown, stirring every 10 minutes.

Allow to cool to room temperature, then break into small pieces, into a large clean bowl. Mix the dried pineapple and puffed quinoa through.

Transfer to a large jar or airtight container and store in the pantry. The granola will keep for up to 1 month.

INGREDIENTS

1 free-range egg white
1 tablespoon cold water
1 tablespoon light-tasting vegetable oil
90 g (3¼ oz/¼ cup) honey
1 teaspoon natural vanilla extract
1 teaspoon sea salt
20 g (¾ oz/¼ cup) shredded coconut
80 g (2¾ oz/½ cup) almonds, roughly chopped
40 g (1½ oz/¼ cup) pepitas (pumpkin seeds)
40 g (1½ oz/¼ cup) sunflower seeds
4 slices dried pineapple, diced
60 g (2¼ oz/1 cup) puffed quinoa, or your favourite puffed grain

Pears and hazelnuts are a classic combination. As with most ingredients that seem to always be seen together, it is because they are at their tastiest in the same season – in this case, autumn. If you buy hazelnuts with the skins still on, quickly roast them for 5–10 minutes in a hot oven and then use a clean tea towel to rub off the skins. I like to add a good whack of ginger to this granola, as it not only tastes great, but the heat it adds provides a good kickstart to my day.

PEAR, HAZELNUT & GINGER GRANOLA

MAKES: 1 x 1 litre (32 oz) jar

INGREDIENTS

1 free-range egg white
1 tablespoon cold water
1 tablespoon light-tasting vegetable oil
90 g (3¼ oz/¼ cup) honey
1 teaspoon natural vanilla extract
1 teaspoon sea salt
1 teaspoon ground cinnamon
145 g (5 oz/1½ cups) rolled (porridge) oats (not the instant or quick-cooking variety)
100 g (3½ oz/½ cup) quinoa
40 g (1½ oz/¼ cup) pepitas (pumpkin seeds)
75 g (2½ oz/½ cup) hazelnuts, skins removed, roughly chopped
135 g (4¾ oz/¾ cup) dried pears, diced
110 g (3¾ oz/½ cup) unsugared crystallised ginger, cut into bite-sized pieces

METHOD

Preheat the oven to 160°C (315°F) and line a large baking tray with baking paper. It's best to use a tray that has sides, so the granola doesn't spill out everywhere.

In a large bowl, whisk together the egg white and water until slightly foamy. Add the oil, honey and vanilla extract and give it a good stir.

Add the rest of the ingredients, except the dried pear and ginger. Stir vigorously with a wooden spoon, making sure all the ingredients are well coated.

Evenly spread the mixture over the lined baking tray, making sure the layer is no more than 1 cm (½ inch) thick, otherwise the granola won't crisp up nicely.

Toast in the oven for 30 minutes, or until golden brown, stirring every 10 minutes.

Allow to cool to room temperature, then break into small pieces, into a large clean bowl. Mix the dried pears and ginger through.

Transfer to a large jar or airtight container and store in the pantry. The granola will keep for up to 1 month.

Try this granola on a cold winter's morning with warm milk and poached pears and you'll be hooked. This is also my favourite granola to make into a healthy crumble with pears, apples or rhubarb. See the recipe on page 20 to learn how.

WALNUT, CINNAMON & DATE GRANOLA

MAKES: 1 x 1 litre (32 oz) jar

METHOD

Preheat the oven to 160°C (315°F) and line a large baking tray with baking paper. It's best to use a tray that has sides, so the granola doesn't spill out everywhere.

In a large bowl, whisk together the egg white and water until slightly foamy. Add the oil, honey and vanilla extract and give it a good stir.

Add the rest of the ingredients, except the dates. Stir vigorously with a wooden spoon, making sure all the ingredients are well coated.

Evenly spread the mixture over the lined baking tray, making sure the layer is no more than 1 cm (½ inch) thick, otherwise the granola won't crisp up nicely.

Toast in the oven for 30 minutes, or until golden brown, stirring every 10 minutes.

Allow to cool to room temperature, then break into small pieces, into a large clean bowl. Mix the dates through.

Transfer to a large jar or airtight container and store in the pantry. The granola will keep for up to 1 month.

INGREDIENTS

1 free-range egg white
1 tablespoon cold water
1 tablespoon light-tasting vegetable oil
90 g (3¼ oz/¼ cup) honey
1 teaspoon natural vanilla extract
1 teaspoon sea salt
2 teaspoons ground cinnamon
190 g (6¾ oz/2 cups) rolled (porridge) oats (not the instant or quick-cooking variety)
100 g (3½ oz/½ cup) quinoa
60 g (2¼ oz/½ cup) walnuts
40 g (1½ oz/¼ cup) sunflower seeds
40 g (1½ oz/¼ cup) pepitas (pumpkin seeds)
135 g (4¾ oz/¾ cup) pitted dried dates, cut into bite-sized pieces

This lovely crumble is light, tasty and wonderfully versatile. Swap the rhubarb for whatever fruits are in season – peaches in summer, plums and pears in autumn, apples in winter. I usually have a crumble on the day I've prepared a big batch of granola, saving a few cups of the uncooked granola mixture to make a quick and easy crumble topping.

AUTUMN GRANOLA CRUMBLE

SERVES 4

INGREDIENTS

1 bunch rhubarb
4 pears
100 g (3½ oz/½ cup, lightly packed) brown sugar
60 g (2¼ oz) butter, at room temperature, chopped
185 g (6½ oz/1½ cups) uncooked granola

METHOD

Preheat the oven to 200°C (400°F).

Give the rhubarb a good rinse, then cut into bite-sized pieces, discarding any green stems. Peel and core the pears, then chop to the same size as the rhubarb. Spread the fruit, sugar and half the butter in a 20 cm (8 inch) baking dish.

Bake for 15–20 minutes, or until the fruit is soft and bubbling in a little bit of syrup.

Remove the baking dish from the oven and spread the uncooked granola on top. Dot with pieces of the remaining butter and bake for a further 5 minutes, or until the granola is nicely golden.

Spoon into bowls and serve warm, with cream, ice cream, Yoghurt (page 95) or Whipped ricotta (page 111).

NUT BUTTER

If there is one project you should try, this is it. Not only because it's so easy, but nut butters are quite expensive to buy and often full of unnecessary oils and preservatives. Grab a handful of nuts or seeds, roast them, blend them with some honey and spices and you'll end up with the most luscious, sweet spread that is just waiting for a thick slice of toast – or, if you are like me, simply a spoon. You can get creative with the combinations (the Pepita and honey butter below is an absolute and unexpected knock-out), but try the simple Almond butter first so you can learn the process.

MAKES: 1 x 280 ml (10 oz) jar

INGREDIENTS

ALMOND BUTTER
320 g (11¼ oz/2 cups) unsalted almonds
1 tablespoon melted coconut oil

CHOCOLATE & MACADAMIA BUTTER
300 g (10½ oz/2 cups) raw
    macadamia nuts
2 tablespoons honey
3 tablespoons good-quality unsweetened
    Dutch-processed cocoa powder
1 teaspoon sea salt
1 tablespoon melted coconut oil

PEPITA & HONEY BUTTER
465 g (1 lb/3 cups) pepitas (pumpkin seeds)
1 teaspoon ground cinnamon
2 teaspoons honey
1 tablespoon melted coconut oil

MAPLE PEANUT BUTTER
280 g (10 oz/2 cups) unsalted
    roasted peanuts
1 teaspoon sea salt
2 tablespoons maple syrup
1 tablespoon melted coconut oil

EQUIPMENT

baking tray lined with baking paper
food processor
spatula
1 x 280 ml (10 oz) jar and lid

NUT BUTTER METHOD

$\left(1\right)$ »

Prepare your oven: Preheat the oven to 160°C (315°F).

Roast the nuts or seeds: Place the almonds, macadamias, pepitas or peanuts in a single layer on a baking tray lined with baking paper. Roast until just golden, but do not let them brown. Almonds will take about 7 minutes, macadamias 10–20 minutes, and pepitas and peanuts about 10 minutes.

Cool and blend: Let them cool slightly, then place in a food processor. Add the remaining ingredients and blend for 5 minutes, or until smooth. Be patient as the nuts or seeds will take the full 5 minutes to transform from powder to crumbs to clumps, and then to a smooth butter. If after 5–7 minutes the butter isn't a lovely smooth paste, add an additional tablespoon of melted coconut oil.

③ Bottle: Using a spatula, scrape your nut or pepita butter out of the food processor, into a clean jar. Screw the lid on tightly. The nut butter will keep on the shelf for up to 1 month, or in the fridge for up to 2 months. If you store it in the fridge, bring it to room temperature before using, to make it easier to spread.

HOW TO USE

- Spread Pepita & honey butter (page 23) thickly on freshly toasted sourdough bread, then top with banana, more honey and some toasted coconut flakes for a decadent breakfast.
- Enrich a banana smoothie with a big tablespoon of Almond butter (page 23), a few dates and a sprinkling of cardamom seeds.
- Swirl through softened ice cream.

Making pancakes started as a Shrove Tuesday tradition in my family. It had very little to do with religious observance and everything to do with consuming a vast amount of pancakes. Being the youngest of six children, I had to fight for my share – a skill I have to this day. This pancake mixture is light and fluffy, and the addition of wattleseed essence gives a lovely nutty flavour, although you can leave it out if you can't get hold of any. Use buttermilk instead of milk if you have some handy; just add a teaspoon of bicarbonate of soda (baking soda) as well.

WATTLESEED PANCAKES WITH NUT BUTTER

MAKES: 6 generously sized pancakes

INGREDIENTS

2 free-range eggs
435 ml (15¼ fl oz/1¾ cups) milk
    or buttermilk
2 tablespoons melted butter
1 teaspoon wattleseed essence
300 g (10½ oz/2 cups) plain
    (all-purpose) flour, sifted
small pinch of sea salt
1 tablespoon sugar
1 teaspoon baking powder
vegetable oil, for pan-frying
Nut butter of your choice (page 23),
    at room temperature, for spreading;
    if it is a little too hard to spread,
    mix in 1 tablespoon melted
    coconut oil or butter

METHOD

Crack the eggs into a small bowl. Add the milk, melted butter and wattleseed essence. Whisk together until well combined.

In a large bowl, combine the flour, salt, sugar and baking powder; if using buttermilk instead of milk, also add 1 teaspoon bicarbonate of soda (baking soda). Add the egg mixture and stir together with a fork until just combined; it's okay if there are a few little lumps. Just don't overmix the batter or you'll end up with tough pancakes.

Cover with plastic wrap and leave to rest; this is a really important step, and will give you a lighter, fluffier pancake. Leave the batter on the bench for an hour or so while you read the paper and have a coffee – or if you're really organised, pop the batter in the fridge to rest overnight.

When ready to serve, heat a large frying pan over medium heat. Add a teaspoon of vegetable oil. When it shimmers, turn the heat down to medium–low and spoon in 125 ml (4 fl oz/½ cup) of the pancake batter. The batter will spread slightly. Resist the urge to flip the pancake until bubbles form on the surface; this should take about 2–3 minutes. Flip and cook for another 2 minutes. Remove and place in a warm oven or cover with a tea towel while making the remaining pancakes, adding more oil to the pan as needed.

Serve warm, topped with nut butter.

CORDIAL

Forget the sickly sweet green and red cordials of your youth. Chock full of artificial colours and flavours and a ridiculous amount of sugar, they belonged more in a science lab than a kitchen pantry. I'm about to show you a world of cordials that will not only knock your socks off, but are dead easy to make, and showcase the best fruits of the season – without the junk.

This lemon and passionfruit flavoured cordial is my go-to drink on a hot day. Nothing says summer like passionfruit; we are blessed to have them growing in abundance where I live. Here is a fantastic way to capture their deliciously tart sweetness. This cordial will keep for a month in the fridge, so you can make it at the end of summer and keep the dream alive into autumn.

Once you get the process down, experiment with different fruit, herbs and spices like pepper. Just use the best-tasting fruit you can find at the height of the season and you'll be well rewarded.

Perfect for a long drink in the afternoon, a dressed-up cocktail or even a frozen ice.

MAKES: 2 x 700 ml (24 fl oz) bottles

INGREDIENTS

500 ml (17 fl oz/2 cups) water
440 g (15½ oz/2 cups) raw sugar
500 ml (17 fl oz/2 cups) lemon juice;
  you'll need about 10 large juicy,
  thin-skinned lemons
250 g (9 oz/1 cup) passionfruit pulp,
  including the seeds; you'll need about
  15 large passionfruit

EQUIPMENT

vegetable peeler
large heavy-based saucepan
sieve
bowl
funnel
2 x 700 ml (24 fl oz) bottles

CORDIAL METHOD

 Make the syrup: Combine the water and sugar in a large heavy-based saucepan. Bring to the boil. When the sugar has dissolved, reduce the heat and leave to simmer for 5 minutes, then remove from the heat and leave to cool.

 Prepare the fruit: Using whatever juicer you have on hand, juice all the lemons; you'll need 500 ml (17 fl oz/2 cups) lemon juice all up. Cut the passionfruit in half and scoop out the pulp, making sure you catch all the juice.

 Mix together: When the syrup has cooled, add the lemon juice and passionfruit pulp. Stir until well combined.

 Bottle and store: Using a funnel, pour the cordial into two clean bottles. Seal and store in the fridge, where the cordial will keep for up to 1 month.

Serve: Serve over ice, with lots of sparkling water.

HOW TO USE

- This cordial and the ones on the following pages are incredibly versatile. They all make a perfect base for cocktails: one-third fill a glass with your chosen cordial, top with a shot of gin, soda water (club soda) and mint, and serve on a hot summer's afternoon.
- Splash a little cordial over a seasonal fruit salad of strawberries, watermelon and grapes in late summer, or apples, pears and persimmon in winter. Serve with ice cream or sweetened Whipped ricotta (page 111).
- Whisk some Ginger cordial (page 34) with olive oil, paprika, garlic, mustard, salt and pepper and use as a marinade for slow-roasted pulled pork.
- Use the Ginger cordial (page 34) in a classic Dark and Stormy. Combine equal parts cordial, soda water (club soda) and dark rum; add a big squeeze of lime juice and crushed ice.
- Add a teaspoon of your favourite cordial to sweeten iced tea.

Blood oranges are one of the most beautiful fruits around. If the frosts are good, the season will be full of juicy oranges with a vibrant red juice, perfect for cordials. The addition of rosemary gives a more complex flavour. If you can't find blood oranges, this cordial works just as well with regular oranges.

BLOOD ORANGE & ROSEMARY CORDIAL

MAKES: 2 x 700 ml (24 fl oz) bottles

INGREDIENTS

500 ml (17 fl oz/2 cups) water
440 g (15½ oz/2 cups) raw sugar
1 small rosemary sprig
500 ml (17 fl oz/2 cups) blood orange
    juice; depending on their size,
    you'll need about 7 oranges
250 ml (9 fl oz/1 cup) lemon juice;
    you'll need about 5 large juicy,
    thin-skinned lemons

METHOD

Combine the water, sugar and rosemary in a large heavy-based saucepan. Bring to the boil. When the sugar has dissolved, reduce the heat and leave to simmer for 5 minutes, then remove from the heat and leave to cool.

Using whatever juicer you have on hand, juice the oranges and lemons.

When the syrup has cooled, remove the rosemary and stir in the blood orange and lemon juice.

Using a funnel, pour the cordial into two clean bottles. Seal and store in the fridge, where the cordial will keep for up to 1 month.

Serve over ice, with lots of sparkling water.

There is nothing punk rock about this ruby red, sweet sparkly cordial. It is perfect for long afternoons, pretty dresses and high tea. The colour is gorgeous and the combination of tart rhubarb and fragrant quince is unbeatable. If quinces aren't in season, you can leave them out and the cordial will still be lovely.

RHUBARB & QUINCE CORDIAL

MAKES: 2 x 700 ml (24 fl oz) bottles

METHOD

Wash the rhubarb, then cut into bite-sized pieces, discarding the leaves and any greener bits of stalk. Peel the zest from the lemon into long strips using a vegetable peeler. Wash, peel and core the quinces, reserving the quince peelings.

Place the fruit, lemon zest, quince peelings, sugar and water in a large heavy-based saucepan and bring to a gentle boil. Cook over low heat until the rhubarb and quince are soft and you can mash them with the back of a wooden spoon; this should take about 20 minutes. Leave to cool and infuse for a few hours, or even overnight in the fridge.

Place a sieve over a bowl and pour in the fruit syrup mixture. Leave to drain for an hour or two.

Once it has drained, scoop the fruit out of the sieve and remove the quince peelings. Keep the rhubarb and quince for serving over Granola (page 12) or pancakes, or to blend into sweet smoothies; be sure to use within the next day or two.

Using a funnel, pour the cordial into two clean bottles. Seal and store in the fridge, where the cordial will keep for up to 1 month.

INGREDIENTS

15 rhubarb stalks
1 lemon
3 quinces
440 g (15½ oz/2 cups) granulated white sugar
1.25 litres (52 fl oz/6 cups) water

It is the sharp bite of ginger that makes this deliciously versatile cordial so irresistible. When you leave the cordial to infuse overnight, try adding extra aromatics such as mint, rosemary, lemongrass, zested lime or lemon peel, or even some black peppercorns. Be sure not to throw away the ginger after you strain it – the leftover bits are perfect for using in chutneys and jams, or to flavour teas, Water kefir (page 164) or Kombucha (page 158).

GINGER CORDIAL

MAKES: 2 x 700 ml (24 fl oz) bottles

INGREDIENTS

15 cm (6 inch) knob of fresh ginger
440 g (15½ oz/2 cups) raw or
    granulated white sugar
1.5 litres (52 fl oz/6 cups) water
3 long strips of lemon peel
juice of 1 lemon

METHOD

Peel the ginger by using a teaspoon or a small sharp knife to scrape away the papery skin. Grate the ginger, or slice thinly using a sharp knife.

In a large saucepan, combine the ginger, sugar, water and lemon peel. Bring to the boil. When the sugar has dissolved, reduce the heat and leave to simmer for 5 minutes.

Turn off the heat, then leave to infuse on the stove overnight, or for at least 5 hours.

Place a fine-mesh sieve, or a colander lined with muslin (cheesecloth), over a large bowl. Pour in the syrup mixture and add the lemon juice to the bowl. Discard the lemon peel; reserve the grated ginger for other uses. The cordial should be syrupy and sweet, with a sharp kick of ginger.

Using a funnel, pour the cordial into two clean bottles. Seal and store in the fridge, where the cordial will keep for up to 1 month.

This cocktail recipe belonged to Hannah Maclurcan, an early celebrity Australian cookbook writer, who also famously ran the old Wentworth Hotel in Sydney during the early decades of the 1900s. The cocktail's arrival in the young colony occurred rather earlier, however, when boats laden with hunks of ice, hauled from the lakes of Boston, first made their way into Sydney Harbour in 1839. The newly arrived settlers, not shy of a drink or two, toasted this momentous occasion with generous rounds of 'cobblers'.

Originally featuring sherry, cobblers are heavy on both booze and ice, sweetened with a dash of cordial or sugar syrup – perfect for a summer's day. Feel free to experiment using brandy, bourbon or rum for the spirits, and other cordial flavours.

I've made it here with bourbon and my Ginger cordial (see opposite page), but don't dare skimp on the straw, or you'll have Hannah to answer to.

GINGER COBBLER

SERVES 4

METHOD

Fill four tumblers three parts full with crushed ice. Pour a tablespoon of cordial into each tumbler and stir together.

Pour the bourbon over and top with more crushed ice. Must be served with a straw.

INGREDIENTS

crushed ice
4 tablespoons Ginger cordial (page 34)
240 ml (8 fl oz) bourbon

PRESERVED GARLIC

I love this project because it's like a two-for-one deal: your garlic cloves are perfectly preserved for months, and you also end up with a jar full of pungent garlicky olive oil that you can use on everything from soft ricotta and tomato on toast, to brushing over meat before cooking it on the barbecue.

The quality of garlic sold in most supermarkets around the world is patchy at best. Those white bulbs are often imported and bleached, which is why they are so clean and bright – not my kind of garlic. When garlic season hits, which is usually late autumn and spring, find the best organic, locally grown cloves you can, then preserve them so you can live like a king for the rest of the year.

MAKES: 1 x 500 ml (16 oz) jar

INGREDIENTS

10 garlic bulbs
1 rosemary sprig
1 small red chilli
1 teaspoon black peppercorns
200 ml (7 fl oz) extra virgin olive oil, approximately
200 ml (7 fl oz) vegetable oil, approximately

EQUIPMENT

knife
medium saucepan
1 x 500 ml (16 oz) jar and lid

PRESERVED GARLIC METHOD

 Prepare the garlic: Break the garlic bulbs into individual cloves. Peel each clove; to make the job easier, gently press each clove with the back of a knife to loosen the skin before peeling. You should end up with about 2 cups of peeled cloves.

 Boil the garlic: Place the garlic cloves in a saucepan and cover with cold water. Bring to the boil, then drain. Repeat this three times. The garlic will soften.

③ Pack the jar: Place the garlic in a clean jar. Add the rosemary, chilli and peppercorns, then pour in the olive oil and vegetable oil, making sure the garlic cloves are covered by at least 2 cm (¾ inch) of oil so they don't spoil; the amount of oil you'll need may vary depending on the size of the garlic cloves. Also, don't be tempted to use only olive oil for packing the garlic cloves, as it will harden in the fridge; using vegetable oil in the mix will keep the oils liquid.

④ Store: Seal and store in the refrigerator. The garlic will keep for up to 3 months in the oil.

HOW TO USE

- Use the cloves in place of fresh garlic when frying your onions and garlic for pasta sauces.
- Add a few cloves and some rosemary to your No-knead bread (page 118).
- The oil is just as delicious as the garlic. When you've used up all the preserved garlic cloves, use the garlicky oil in place of regular oil when marinating olives, brush it on vegetables before grilling, or use as a marinade for meats.
- Make a sensational garlic roast chicken by stuffing the cloves under the skin with some chopped rosemary, then brushing the whole chicken with the oil.

PRESERVED PEARS

When I first wanted to start preserving fruit, I thought I'd need a kitchen filled with boxes of fruit, kilos of sugar and hundreds of jars. Unless you have an army of helpers, an easier way is to just bottle a few kilos of fruit at a time, so you don't end up with mountains of the same preserve, and can experiment with different flavours.

This recipe will give you several jars of sweetly aromatic pears. You can easily substitute other fruits such as plums, nectarines and peaches, or add different aromatics to the jars, such as orange zest, cardamom, rosemary, or even chilli.

MAKES: 4 x 500 ml (16 oz) jars

INGREDIENTS

½ lemon
1.2 kg (2 lb 10 oz) pears
100 g (3½ oz) raw or granulated white sugar
700 ml (24 fl oz) water
16 black peppercorns
2 star anise, broken in half
1 cinnamon stick, broken into 4 pieces

EQUIPMENT

4 x 500 ml (16 oz) wide-mouthed jars and lids
vegetable peeler
bowl
medium saucepan
large saucepan
preserving tongs (optional)
tea towels
sugar thermometer

PRESERVED PEARS METHOD

 1 **Prepare your jars:** Sterilise your jars and lids using a method outlined on page 55. Keep them warm until you are ready to use them.

 2 **Peel the fruit:** Squeeze the juice from the lemon half into a bowl of water. Peel, core and quarter the pears, placing them into the lemon water as you go, to stop them turning brown.

 3 **Make your syrup:** In a medium saucepan, gently heat the sugar and water until the sugar has dissolved.

 4 **Pack your jars:** Pack the pears into the warm jars, tucking them in really tight, otherwise they will float around when you add the syrup; any fruit that is exposed to air will encourage mould. Divide the pepper, cinnamon and star anise among the jars.

 5 **Fill and seal:** Pour the warm syrup over the pears. Tap the jars gently to make sure there are no air bubbles. Clean the rims with paper towel, making sure they are spotless, and carefully screw the lids on, making sure they're not too tight.

6 **Boil the jars:** Grab your biggest saucepan, place a tea towel in the bottom and fill with water. Bring to the boil, then add your jars, making sure they are not touching each other. Simmer at 88°C (190°F) for 40 minutes. This will pasteurise the jars and prevent spoilage.

 7 **Cool and store:** After 40 minutes, carefully lift the jars out using preserving tongs and place on a tea towel on your bench. (If you don't have preserving tongs, you can leave the jars to cool in the water.) Don't touch the jars until they are completely cool. Store in a dark cupboard for up to 1 year.

HOW TO USE

- Serve with ice cream or mascarpone and chocolate sauce for a quick, easy dessert.
- Rest your beautiful pears atop a simple sweet tart base filled with custard and chocolate shavings or Cheat's ricotta (page 104).
- Perfect with your home-made Granola (page 12) for a decadent breakfast.

MUSTARD

Making mustard is so simple, you really will ask yourself, 'Is that all there is?' Waiting to enjoy the fruits of your labour may test your patience, though, because mustard needs time to rest before you can eat it. And by rest, I mean a month, or even two. The flavours are really intense to start with, and you might even think you've done something wrong – but with some time on the shelf, the flavours mellow out, and you'll be spreading your mustard onto toasted cheese sandwiches, dolloping it on hot dogs, or stirring it into tangy salad dressings with great satisfaction.

MAKES: 1 x 280 ml (10 oz) jar

INGREDIENTS

85 g (3 oz/½ cup) brown mustard seeds
125 ml (4 fl oz/½ cup) cold water
50 g (1¾ oz/½ cup) yellow
   mustard powder
125 ml (4 fl oz/½ cup) white wine vinegar
1½ teaspoons sea salt
1 teaspoon ground turmeric

EQUIPMENT

small or large bowl
upright blender
spatula or spoon
1 x 280 ml (10 oz) jar and lid

MUSTARD METHOD

 Soak the seeds: Put the mustard seeds in a small bowl, cover with the cold water and leave to soak overnight.

 Prepare your jar: The next day, sterilise your jar and lid, using a method outlined on page 55.

 Blend: Drain the mustard seeds and place in an upright blender. Add the mustard powder and blend for 30 seconds, then leave to rest for 10 minutes. Now add the vinegar, salt and turmeric and blend to a smooth paste.

 Pack your jar: Spoon the mustard into your sterilised jar, tapping gently to remove all the air bubbles. Screw the lid on firmly.

 Store then eat: Leave in a dark place for 4–6 weeks, or until the flavours have mellowed. Don't be tempted to eat it sooner as it will taste bitter. Once opened, keep in the fridge and use within 2 months.

HOW TO USE

- Serve on top of grilled meats and sausages at your next barbecue.
- No roast beef sandwich is quite right unless it has lots of butter, a good spread of mustard and some spicy greens such as rocket (arugula).
- Whisk a teaspoon of mustard with a tablespoon of melted butter and serve over steamed asparagus.
- Make a simple marinade with mustard, olive oil, lemon juice, crushed bay leaves and garlic.
- Combine mustard with room-temperature butter, oregano and a pinch of sea salt. Stuff under the breast skin of a free-range chicken before roasting.
- Make a mustard cream dressing with red wine vinegar, mustard and sour cream for an amazing potato salad.
- Salad dressing is always better with mustard. Add a teaspoon to equal amounts of extra virgin olive oil and apple cider vinegar or lemon juice, then season with sea salt and freshly ground black pepper and whisk well. Dress your salad just before serving.

The addition of beer to this mustard gives it a lovely earthy taste. Use your favourite local beer, but stick to the lighter tasting ales or lagers.

PALE ALE MUSTARD

MAKES: 1 x 280 ml (10 oz) jar

INGREDIENTS

85 g (3 oz/½ cup) yellow
    mustard seeds
85 g (3 oz/½ cup) brown
    mustard seeds
250 ml (9 fl oz/1 cup) pale ale
1 tablespoon sea salt
85 ml (2¾ fl oz) apple cider vinegar
90 g (3¼ oz/¼ cup) honey
1 tablespoon ground nutmeg

METHOD

In a large bowl, combine the mustard seeds and beer. Cover and set aside overnight. The mustard seeds will swell up, soften and soak up most of the beer.

The next day, sterilise a small jar and its lid, using a method outlined on page 55.

Transfer the mustard seeds and beer to an upright blender. Add the salt, vinegar, honey and nutmeg, then blend until nearly smooth.

Spoon the mustard into your sterilised jar, tapping gently to remove all the air bubbles. Screw the lid on firmly.

Leave in a dark place for 2–6 weeks, or until the flavours have mellowed. Don't be tempted to eat it sooner as it will taste bitter. Once opened, keep in the fridge and use within 2 months.

This is a lovely way to spice up mayonnaise. Use on a traditional hot dog, alongside grilled fish, or on a crunchy bread roll stuffed with shredded poached chicken and spicy salad greens.

YELLOW MUSTARD SAUCE WITH TARRAGON

MAKES: 1 x 280 ml (10 oz) jar

METHOD

Add all the ingredients to a large mixing bowl and stir with a wooden spoon until well blended.

Spoon into a small clean jar, screw the lid on and leave in the fridge overnight for the flavours to develop. Keep in the fridge and use within 3–5 days.

INGREDIENTS

90 g (3¼ oz/⅓ cup) Mustard (page 45)
60 ml (2 fl oz/¼ cup) red wine vinegar
2 tablespoons finely chopped tarragon leaves
1 teaspoon lemon juice
½ teaspoon sweet paprika
¼ teaspoon sea salt
235 g (8½ oz/1 cup) mayonnaise
¼ teaspoon ground white pepper

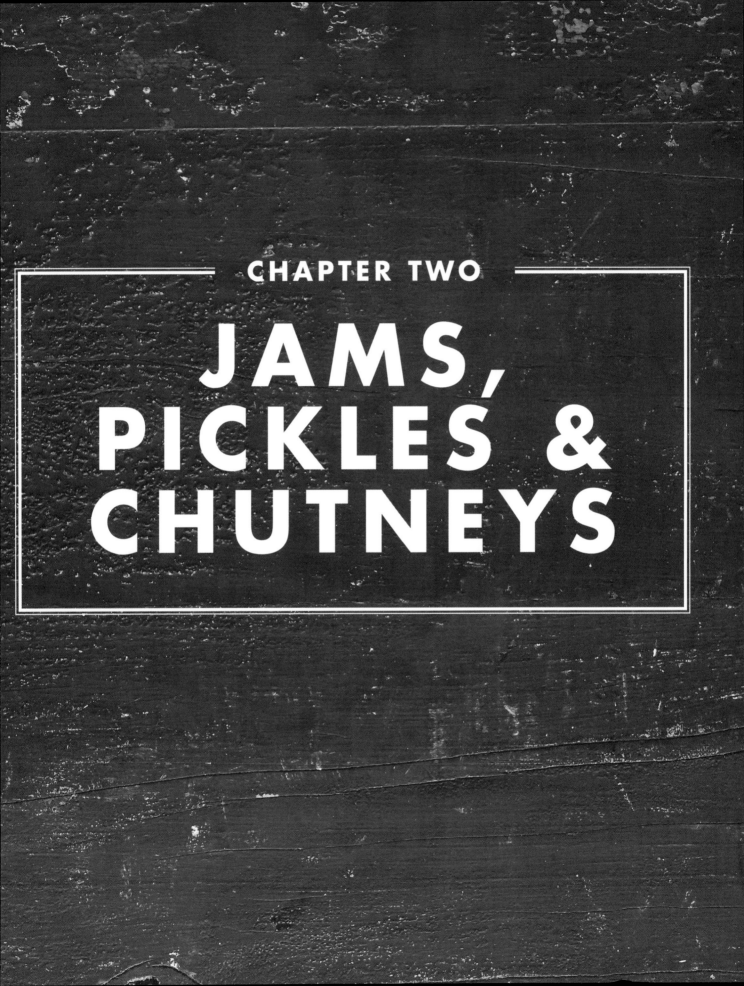

CHAPTER TWO

JAMS, PICKLES & CHUTNEYS

JAM 101

I spent years avoiding making jam because I thought I would need to set aside a full day, make a trip to the market for some huge boxes of fruit and clean thousands of jars, which frankly all seemed way too hard. But the moment I learnt to make small batches of jam, everything changed. Now I grab a few punnets of berries when they're on sale, open a bag of sugar, and in less than 45 minutes I have a couple of warm jars full of sweet jam, a cup of tea in my hand, and a satisfied look on my face. It's that easy. Here are a few things you need to know if you are going to get into making jam.

THE HOLY TRINITY

Pectin, sugar and **acid** are the holy trinity when making jam. Without all three, your jam won't set and you will end up with a sauce, albeit a delicious one.

Pectin occurs naturally in varying amounts in all fruits, with berries having a small amount, and tart fruits such as apples and plums having more. When pectin is combined with an acid (like lemon juice) and sugar, it forms a jelly, which is how the jam sets.

Most traditional jams call for white sugar, but when you get the hang of making jam, try experimenting with different sugars. I often use a mix of one-third brown sugar to two-thirds white sugar, to give the jam a darker hue and a light caramel taste. Pale sugars are generally lighter in flavour, while darker sugars such as brown, demerara or raw sugar give a stronger flavour.

If you are nervous about getting your jam to set, you can also buy sugar that has pectin added (such as JamSetta). It can be found in supermarkets and used in place of sugar in most jam recipes.

PICK THE BEST FRUIT

To give your jam the best chance of setting easily, make sure you use slightly under-ripe or perfectly ripe fruit, as it contains useful levels of pectin. Overripe fruit is not great for jam, as it is naturally low in pectin, so leave it for stewing. When you're planning on making jam, hit up your local farmers' market and see what fruit is cheap, plentiful and in season.

ABOUT YOUR JARS

There are as many types of jars you can use as there are jams you can make. My preference is for the American Ball mason jars because they are solid, never break, and I can always get replacement lids as they are a standard size. You can use any good-quality jar, even a second-hand one, as long as it has a new lid, or intact seal, and is properly sterilised.

STERILISING YOUR JARS AND BOTTLES

There are four main ways to sterilise your jars. Be sure to time your sterilising well, so the jars are at the right temperature for the contents. The rule of thumb is to put warm contents such as jams and chutneys into warm jars, and cool contents such as brines into cool jars. If you don't follow these rules, your jars will crack and all your hard work will be undone.

Also make sure all your other utensils (such as ladles, spoons and funnels) are spotlessly clean and dry.

Boiling: Place your jars and lids in a large pot, cover with water and bring to the boil. Turn off the heat and leave in the water until you need to use them. Be very careful when retrieving your jars as they will be hot and full of boiling water. (I highly recommend investing in a pair of preserving tongs designed for the purpose, as it will make it much easier and safer to handle hot jars and lids; you can buy these from kitchenware shops.) Place your drained jars and lids onto a clean tea towel on your kitchen bench until you are ready to use them.

Dishwasher: Put your jars and lids through a hot wash cycle at 65°C (150°F). Leave to air dry.

Baby bottle steriliser: A slightly unconventional way to sterilise your jars, but very effective. You can pick up second-hand electric baby bottle sterilisers quite easily, and they are great for small-batch preserving. In a matter of minutes you can have two to four sterilised jars, and they will stay warm until you need them.

Oven: Heat your oven to 150°C (300°F). Wash your jars in hot soapy water and rinse them, then place in the heated oven for 30 minutes. Turn the oven off and let them sit there until you are ready to use them.

CHECKING FOR SETTING POINT

Here are three surefire ways of testing if your jam has set.

Sugar thermometer: This is the method I use. The jam will have reached setting point when it registers 104°C (220°F) on a sugar thermometer, which you can buy inexpensively from kitchenware shops.

Wooden spoon: Dip a wooden spoon into the jam and slowly remove it. If the jam isn't ready, it will run off the spoon in a single thin drip. If it is ready, it will slowly form two thick drips.

The wrinkle test: Place a saucer or metal spoon in the freezer. When you think you are near setting point, take it out and place a small amount of jam onto it. Pop it back into the freezer for a minute, then push the jam with your finger. If the jam wrinkles on the surface, it is done. If your batch of jam refuses to set after cooling, tip it back into the pan, add some more lemon juice and bring back to the boil for another 5 minutes or so.

SEALING YOUR JARS

There is no sweeter sound than freshly potted jam jars sealing. You'll hear a little 'pop', and then you'll know that the jar has vacuum-sealed and your precious cargo is safe inside. Test by pressing on the lid – it should be concave and firm. You can then leave the jars in a dark cupboard for up to 6 months.

If any of your jars haven't sealed properly, store them in the fridge and use within 2 weeks.

ANY BERRY JAM

This is the quickest route from fruit to jam you'll find, because with berries there is no need to take out stones or pits, or peel or chop anything. Too easy! This is why berry jam is a good one to start with. Whenever you see berries on sale, grab a few punnets and cook up a few jars. You can use a mix of berries, or stick to just one kind.

The amount of sugar you need really depends on how sweet the fruit is, but a good rule of thumb is to use 1 part sugar to 2 parts fruit. Your yield will also depend on how large and juicy your fruit is, so don't worry if you only get one jar that is half full. It will keep in the fridge for up to a month.

There are so many additions that will really transform this simple jam. I often add a vanilla bean for extra sweetness, or a tablespoon of balsamic vinegar, which makes the flavour more complex. You could also add a few shredded kaffir lime leaves, or some spices such as cinnamon sticks or a star anise.

MAKES: 3 x 280 ml (10 oz) jars

INGREDIENTS

1 kg (2 lb 4 oz) berries
500 g (1 lb 2 oz) sugar
juice of ½ lemon
2 long strips of lemon peel

EQUIPMENT

large bowl
heavy-based saucepan
3 x 280 ml (10 oz) jars and lids
ladle
wide-mouthed funnel (optional)
paper towel

ANY BERRY JAM METHOD

« (1)

Wash the fruit: Wash and de-stem the berries.

Combine fruit and sugar: Place the berries and sugar in a bowl and leave for at least 2 hours, or overnight. This will draw all of the juice out of the berries and reduce the need to add any water. You can skip this step if you want to get started straight away; just add a tablespoon of water when you start to cook the fruit.

Prepare your jars: Sterilise your jars and lids using a method outlined on page 55. Keep them warm until you are ready to use them.

 »

Cook to setting point: Place the berry and sugar mixture in a heavy-based saucepan, along with the lemon juice and lemon peel. Stir over low heat until the sugar has dissolved. It is important to dissolve all the sugar before the mixture reaches a rolling boil, otherwise it will be difficult to set and the jam may taste too sugary when finished. Cook over medium–high heat until you reach a setting point (see page 55); this will take 15–30 minutes, depending on how juicy your fruit is. If there is any scum on the surface of the jam, just remove with a spoon or stir it back in.

③ ≫

Ladle into your warm jars:
Carefully ladle into warm, sterilised
jars, through a funnel if you have
one, leaving a 1 cm (½ inch) gap
at the top of each jar.

≪ ④

Clean the rims: Using paper towel, clean the rims of the
jars of any jam splatters, screw the lids on and leave until cool.

Eat or store: Eat straight away, or store in a cool dark place
for up to 6 months.

HOW TO USE

- Slather on sourdough toast with a serious amount of butter.
- Layer between two sponge cakes and top with cream for
  a classic afternoon tea.
- When making bread and butter pudding, thickly spread
  some jam on your bread before baking the pudding.
- If you add some peppercorns, the jam will be a little more
  savoury and makes a great addition to a cheese plate.

This is the perfect no-fail jam for aspiring jam makers. Plums are high in pectin, so you are certain to get a good set. I've spiced the jam with cinnamon and star anise, but you can leave these out and it will taste just as good – or experiment with your own spices, such as cardamom, vanilla or even a hint of chilli. As with most jams, the yield will depend on how large and juicy your fruit is. If you are left with half a jar, just pop it in the fridge, where it will keep for up to 1 month.

PLUM JAM

MAKES: 3 x 280 ml (10 oz) jars

INGREDIENTS

1.5 kg (3 lb 5 oz) plums
500 ml (17 fl oz/2 cups) water
1 cinnamon stick
1 star anise
700 g (1 lb 9 oz) sugar

METHOD

Sterilise your jars and lids using a method outlined on page 55. Keep them warm until you are ready to use them.

Take the stones out of the plums and discard. Chop the flesh into bite-sized pieces and place in a heavy-based saucepan. Add the water and spices. Bring to the boil, then reduce the heat and simmer gently until the skins are soft; this should take about 10–15 minutes, depending on how ripe the fruit is.

Pour in the sugar, give it a good stir until the sugar has dissolved, then simmer for 15–30 minutes, or until your jam reaches setting point (see page 55). The jam should be nice and thick, a deep purple colour, and smell sweet and jammy. Remove from the heat and take out the cinnamon stick and star anise.

Carefully ladle into warm, sterilised jars, through a funnel if you have one, leaving a 1 cm (½ inch) gap at the top of each jar. Using paper towel, clean the rims of the jars of any splatters of jam, screw the lids on and leave until cool.

Eat straight away, or store in a cool dark place for up to 6 months.

HOW TO USE

- After frying a duck breast, add some jam to the pan and deglaze with red wine for a plum sauce.
- Combine with a little sherry vinegar, cloves, allspice and cinnamon to glaze a ham.

Quince is the first fruit tree I remember seeing as a kid. This fruit stuck in my memory not because of its odd, knobbly shape or the soft down on its pale yellow skin, but for its unexpected fragrance. Sweet, musty and delicate all at once, the perfume is unmistakable and one of my favourites. The fruit, which you'll find in autumn, is tricky to work with, but well worth the effort, as the hard flesh transforms into a ruby-hued jam worthy of any scone. It's also great on buttered sourdough, or a cheese platter with sharp crumbly cheddar.

QUINCE & CHAMOMILE JAM

MAKES: 3 x 280 ml (10 oz) jars

METHOD

Sterilise your jars and lids using a method outlined on page 55. Keep them warm until you are ready to use them.

Using a tea bag or tea leaves, make a cup of chamomile tea and leave to cool.

Carefully cut the quinces into quarters and remove the core and skin from each piece. Quinces can be tricky to peel, so take care; also, make sure the core is fully removed, or you'll have a grainy jam. Chop into bite-sized pieces and place in a large glass bowl, squeezing in the lemon juice as you go, to stop the quince browning.

Add the quince, water and chamomile tea to a large heavy-based saucepan and bring to a full boil until the quince is slightly softened. Once the fruit has begun to break down and is somewhat translucent, which may take 20–30 minutes depending on how ripe the fruit is, smash the chunks down further using the back of a wooden spoon.

Stir in the sugar. Once it has dissolved, turn the heat down to medium. Cook, stirring frequently, until your jam reaches setting point (see page 55); this should take about 30 minutes. Watch the jam carefully because it has a tendency to stick towards the end. It should be a lovely dark rosy colour and very thick.

Carefully ladle into your warm, sterilised jars, leaving a 1 cm (½ inch) gap at the top of each jar. Using paper towel, clean the rims of the jars of any jam splatters, screw the lids on and leave until cool.

Eat straight away, or store for up to 6 months.

INGREDIENTS

1 chamomile tea bag, or 2 tablespoons chamomile tea leaves
5–6 quinces (about 8 cups chopped quince flesh)
juice of 1 lemon
1.75 litres (61 fl oz/7 cups) water
660 g (1 lb 7½ oz/3 cups) sugar

A delicious jam that makes the most of my favourite summer fruits. Find the best-quality peaches – white or yellow are both fine to use – and make sure they are not over-ripe, or the jam won't set easily. Add the juice and seeds of tart passionfruit and you'll capture the quintessential taste of summer for the rest of the year.

The yield for this jam will differ, depending on the size of your peaches.

PEACH, PASSIONFRUIT & GINGER JAM

MAKES: 3 x 280 ml (10 oz) jars

INGREDIENTS

1 kg (2 lb 4 oz) just-ripe peaches
    (about 7–8 peaches)
10 passionfruit
600 g (1 lb 5 oz/2¾ cups) granulated
    white sugar
100 g (3½ oz/½ cup, lightly packed)
    brown sugar
4 slices of fresh ginger
juice of ½ lemon

METHOD

Sterilise your jars and lids using a method outlined on page 55. Keep them warm until you are ready to use them.

Using a sharp knife, cut the peaches in half. Discard the stones, then peel away the skins. Roughly chop the flesh and place in a large heavy-based saucepan. Cut each passionfruit in half, scoop out the pulp using a spoon, and add to the pan.

Add the remaining ingredients. Place over low heat until the juices start coming out of the fruit and the sugar starts dissolving, then turn the heat up to medium and continue cooking until setting point is reached (see page 55). This could take anywhere from 15–40 minutes, depending on how ripe the peaches are. Remove from the heat and discard the ginger slices.

Carefully ladle into warm, sterilised jars (through a funnel if you have one), leaving a 1 cm (½ inch) gap at the top of each jar. Using paper towel, clean the rims of the jars of any splatters of jam, then screw on the lids and leave until cool.

Eat straight away, or store in a cool dark place for up to 6 months.

This recipe was given to me by my friend Rebecca Sullivan, who is an amazing cook and lover of old recipes and granny skills. It makes a bright, rosy-coloured jam that is quite sweet. In Australia, rosella flowers are available at good farmers' markets in summer through to autumn. Note that there is no lemon in this recipe, as the pectin needed to set the jam comes from the rosella pods.

ROSELLA JAM

MAKES: 4 x 250 ml (8 oz) jars

METHOD

Sterilise your jars and lids using a method outlined on page 55. Keep them warm until you are ready to use them.

Remove and reserve the flowers (the hibiscus-looking petals) from the rosellas. Separate and reserve the harder green-red petals (calyces) from the seedpods. Wash the pods and petals separately. Put both types of petals in a large saucepan and set aside.

Put the pods in a medium heavy-based saucepan, cover generously with water and bring to the boil. Leave to boil, uncovered, for about 30 minutes. Now strain the juice directly onto the petals in the large saucepan.

Bring the petals and juice slowly to the boil, stirring often. Boil for about 20 minutes, or until pulpy – the mixture will reduce substantially.

Measure the pulp and add 220 g (7¾ oz/1 cup) sugar for each cup of pulp. Dissolve the sugar with the pulp over low heat, then bring the mixture back to the boil. Leave to boil rapidly for 20 minutes, or until setting point is reached (see page 55).

Carefully ladle into warm, sterilised jars (through a funnel if you have one), leaving a 1 cm (½ inch) gap at the top of each jar. Using paper towel, clean the rims of the jars of any jam splatters, screw the lids on and leave until cool.

Eat straight away, or store in a cool dark place for up to 6 months.

INGREDIENTS

2 kg (2 lb 4 oz) rosella flowers
220 g (7¾ oz/1 cup) white sugar per cup of rosella pulp

Clockwise from top left: Plum jam (page 60); Butter (page 90); Quince & chamomile jam (page 61); No-knead bread (page 118); Peach, passionfruit & ginger jam (page 62); Any berry jam (page 56).

PICKLES 101

There is a reason every culture in the world has its own version of a pickle. Sharp and sometimes a little sweet, pickles can elevate almost any meal in a second. Imagine a ham sandwich without mustard pickles, sushi without ginger, rice with no kim chi, or a spicy Indian curry lacking the tang of a good sweet mango chutney.

If you are a novice, start with the quick pickles, such as the Farmers' market pickles on page 71, or the Quick cucumber pickles on page 76, to get the hang of it. Just make sure you always use vegetables in perfect condition, and that you are fastidious with sterilising your jars and utensils (see page 55). Also, never go overboard with your spices, as they become more pungent with time. I've ruined many a pickle with heavy-handed spicing.

Three common preserving ingredients used in pickling are vinegar, salt and sugar. The varieties you use will affect the final flavour of your pickles, so here's a quick run-down.

VINEGAR

Pickles rely on vinegar as the main preserving agent, as vinegar contains acetic acid, which inhibits mould. Every vinegar has its own flavour characteristics, so if you want to substitute another vinegar, just be aware you will get a different outcome.

For example, apple cider vinegar retains a taste of apple, giving it a touch of sweetness, whereas red wine vinegar is a little more tannic. I much prefer the depth of flavour from a good-quality apple cider vinegar and avoid using distilled white vinegar, as I think it is too harsh.

Here are my favourite vinegars to use, plus the ones to steer clear of for pickling.

White wine vinegar: Made from white grapes, this can be expensive, so I like to buy it in bulk as it is more economical. It has a great mild flavour.

Red wine vinegar: Made from red wine grapes, this dark-coloured vinegar is the big brother to white wine vinegar. Bolder and darker, it will knock your socks off. Use this when you want a more intensely flavoured pickle, such as pickled grapes.

Apple cider vinegar: Used a lot in American pickling, for its lovely fruity flavour.

Rice wine vinegar: This lightly flavoured variety is used in Asian pickles that have a short marinating time and are kept refrigerated.

Malt vinegar: Typically light brown, malt vinegar is often used in fish and chip shops, but rarely used in pickling as it has a very strong flavour. You will find it used in some chutneys, however.

Sherry and balsamic vinegar: These vinegars are not routinely used in pickling because of both their price and their intensity of flavour. Save these for beautiful salad dressings instead.

SALT

Salt acts as a preserving agent in pickling, as well as drawing out the moisture from the vegetables and keeping your pickles crisp. Always use the type of salt specified in the recipe, because you'll find that if you measure out 1 tablespoon of various salts such as sea salt, rock salt and table salt, you'll get a different result, as each of these salts varies in texture and intensity. There are three main types of salt.

Sea salt: Made from evaporated sea water, this is the salt I always use. It comes as rock salt, finely ground, or flakes. Try using the fine sea salt, as it dissolves easily and has a more consistent spoon measurement.

Kosher salt: Used mainly in American recipes, this salt is named for its use in koshering meat. It has a uniform grain and contains no caking agents. It is great to use because it gives you a consistent measurement, so there is no need to weigh it, and has no clouding effect. If you can't find kosher salt, use finely ground sea salt.

Iodised salt or table salt: This salt includes iodine and caking agents, so it is never used for pickling. The iodine oxidises what you are pickling, turning it an unappetising brown, and makes the mixture cloudy.

SUGAR

Different types of sugar have a significant effect on the taste of your pickles. Pale sugars are lighter in flavour and used for clear pickles. Darker sugars such as brown, demerara or raw sugar are best for thick pickles and chutneys, as they give a lovely caramel taste.

FARMERS' MARKET PICKLES

Here's a great pickling project for beginners – especially if you are lazy, like me. Simple to make, these pickles live in the fridge, so you don't even have to sterilise your jars. I use our weekly leftover vegetables in these pickles, but you can grab pretty much any vegetable, throw it in a jar with some vinegar, water and salt and then keep it in the fridge. It's that simple.

Below I've included a list of vegetables as a guide, but your best bet is to head to a farmers' market and see what's in season. I often top up the pickles during the week with vegetables such as carrots, fennel or celery; in the photo, we've used heirloom carrots.

The pickles keep in the fridge for about a month, after which I find the brine gets too strong and I start again.

MAKES: 1 x 2 litre (64 oz) jar

INGREDIENTS

1 kg (2 lb 4 oz) various vegetables, such as fennel, radish, capsicum (pepper), cucumbers, onions, cauliflower or carrots (heirloom varieties work well)
500 ml (17 fl oz/2 cups) apple cider vinegar (5% acidity)
500 ml (17 fl oz/2 cups) water
2 tablespoons fine sea salt
1 fresh dill sprig
2 teaspoons black peppercorns
1 dried red chilli (optional)
3 fresh or dried bay leaves (optional)

EQUIPMENT

measuring cups
1 x 2 litre (64 oz) glass jar and lid
small saucepan
chopstick
paper towel

FARMERS' MARKET PICKLES METHOD

Prepare your vegetables: Cut your vegetables into bite-sized pieces, or to fit the height of your jars; if using heirloom carrots, trim them and cut the smaller ones in half lengthways, and any larger ones into quarters. (If you use purple carrots, note that the colour will bleed into the brine and turn it pink!)

« ②

Prepare your jar: Wash your jar in very hot soapy water, then rinse well and air dry. There is no need to properly sterilise the jar, as these pickles will be kept in the fridge.

Heat the brine: Place the vinegar, water and salt in a small stainless steel saucepan and bring to the boil, then leave to cool slightly.

Pack the jar: Tightly pack the vegetables into the jar, along with the dill sprig and peppercorns, and the chilli and bay leaves, if using.

Pour in the brine: Now fill the jar with the brine, covering all the vegetables, and leaving at least 1 cm (½ inch) at the top of the jar. Using a chopstick, gently poke the vegetables to make sure there are no air pockets.

≪ (4)

Clean: Wipe the rim of the jar with paper towel.

Put in the fridge: Seal the lid tightly and leave in the fridge.

Eat: Your pickles will be ready to eat within 24 hours, but taste best after a few days.

HOW TO USE

- Serve alongside strong cheddar cheese, leg ham, butter and a stack of fresh sourdough bread for a ploughman's lunch.
- Blend a teaspoon of the brine with dill and mayonnaise to make a delicious dressing for hot dogs and smoked meats.
- Spread some hearty bread with Mustard (page 45), then pile it with roast beef, cheddar cheese and a sprinkling of your chopped pickles.
- Add a shot of the brine to a strong Bloody Mary mix for extra tang.

These are the pickles of my childhood. We had them on our ham and cheese sandwiches, and every bite brings back memories of backyard cricket, red cordial, sunburn and being tormented by my four older brothers. Needless to say, I still make them regularly. You can use either Lebanese cucumbers or zucchini (courgettes) – whatever is cheapest at the markets.

BREAD & BUTTER PICKLES

MAKES: 3 x 500 ml (16 oz) jars

INGREDIENTS

1 kg (2 lb 4 oz) Lebanese (short) cucumbers or small zucchini (courgettes)
1 white onion
1½ tablespoons fine sea salt
875 ml (30 fl oz/3½ cups) apple cider vinegar
100 g (3½ oz) caster (superfine) sugar
1 tablespoon yellow mustard seeds
¼ teaspoon celery seeds
½ teaspoon ground turmeric

METHOD

Using a sharp knife, cut your cucumbers into rounds about 5 mm (¼ inch) thick. Peel and cut the onion in half, then slice thinly.

Place the vegetables in a large bowl, cover with cold water and stir in the salt. This step is important to draw out the excess water in the cucumbers, so they stay crisp in the pickle. Leave for 3 hours or overnight in the fridge. Rinse and drain well.

Sterilise your jars and lids using a method outlined on page 55. Keep them warm until you are ready to use them.

Combine the vinegar, sugar and spices in a medium-sized saucepan over low heat. Once the sugar has dissolved, add the drained cucumber mixture and leave to cool slightly.

Carefully ladle into the warm jars, leaving a 1 cm (½ inch) gap at the top of each jar. Using paper towel, wipe the rims clean. Gently tap to make sure there are no air bubbles, then screw the lids on and leave to cool. The pickles will keep in the pantry for up to 6 months. Once opened, store in the fridge.

HOW TO USE

- Great on a burger with a big dollop of Mustard (page 45) and your favourite melted cheese.
- Stack rye bread with thin slices of corned beef, cheese, your pickles and some Sauerkraut (page 140) for a classic Reuben sandwich.

I have a growing collection of dog-eared cookbooks that I've picked up from charity shops around the country, full of lovely old recipes like syllabub and scones. I can guarantee that nearly every one of them has a recipe for sweet, spicy mustard pickles. A perfect partner for thickly sliced white bread spread with lots of fresh butter and topped with sliced leg ham and sharp cheddar, this pickle is a staple in my household. It takes a while to make, but is well worth the effort.

SWEET MUSTARD PICKLES

MAKES: 4 x 500 ml (16 oz) jars

METHOD

Cut the cucumbers and cauliflower into bite-sized pieces. Quarter the onions. Add the vegetables to a large bowl and cover with cold water. Stir in the 35 g (1¼ oz/¼ cup) of sea salt and let stand in the refrigerator overnight.

The next day, drain and rinse the vegetables and place them in a large heavy-based saucepan.

Sterilise your jars and lids using a method outlined on page 55. Keep them warm until you are ready to use them.

Dice the capsicum and add to the vegetable mixture in the saucepan. Pour in the vinegar and bring to a simmer, then add the sugar and stir until dissolved. Stir in the turmeric, garam masala, celery seeds, ginger and mustard powder.

In a teacup or small bowl, combine the flour with some of the vinegar from the pan and stir until it becomes a very thin paste. (If it is too thick, it will turn into little dumplings, which is not what you want.) Stir the paste back into the pan, then simmer for about 15 minutes, or until the mixture thickens. It should be thick and chunky, and a lovely, deep yellow.

Add the extra 2 teaspoons of salt and adjust to taste. Remove from the heat and allow to cool in the pan for 15 minutes.

Carefully ladle into the warm jars, leaving a 1 cm (½ inch) gap at the top of each jar. Wipe the rims clean with paper towel, screw the lids on and leave to cool. The pickles will keep in the pantry for up to 6 months. Once opened, store in the fridge.

INGREDIENTS

2 Lebanese (short) cucumbers
½ cauliflower
250 g (9 oz) small pearl onions
35 g (1¼ oz/¼ cup) fine sea salt, plus an extra 2 teaspoons
½ red capsicum (pepper)
900 ml (31 fl oz) apple cider vinegar
220 g (7¾ oz/1 cup) raw or granulated white sugar
1 teaspoon ground turmeric
1 teaspoon garam masala
1 teaspoon celery seeds
1 teaspoon ground ginger
2 teaspoons mild mustard powder, such as Keen's
75 g (2½ oz/½ cup) plain (all-purpose) flour

Whenever I see kirby cucumbers at my greengrocer, I always buy a few kilos because they are hands-down the best cucumbers for this recipe. They're about 7–10 cm (2¾–4 inches) long, with a ridged skin and uneven green colour. They are an ugly fruit, but make an excellent pickle because they stay crunchy due to their lower water content and thick, rough skin. Ask your greengrocer to order some in early summer if you can't find any.

You could also use small Lebanese (short) cucumbers for these pickles, but it is a good idea to slice them and salt them overnight to extract as much water as possible, so they don't become soft in the brine.

QUICK CUCUMBER PICKLES

MAKES: 4 x 500 ml (16 oz) jars

INGREDIENTS

1 kg (2 lb 4 oz) kirby cucumbers, or salted and rinsed small Lebanese (short) cucumbers
500 ml (17 fl oz/2 cups) apple cider vinegar
500 ml (17 fl oz/2 cups) water
2 tablespoons kosher salt or sea salt
1 teaspoon black peppercorns
2 garlic cloves, peeled and cut in half
2 fresh dill sprigs
2 small red chillies (optional)

METHOD

Sterilise your jars and lids using a method outlined on page 55. Keep them warm until you are ready to use them.

Wash and dry the cucumbers, being sure to remove any stems or flowers. Either slice the cucumbers into batons, making sure they are the right length to stand up in your jars, or slice them into rounds; you can also leave them whole, if you like.

Combine the vinegar, water and salt in a small saucepan and bring to the boil. Once the salt has dissolved, take the pan off the heat.

Divide the peppercorns, garlic, dill and chillies, if using, among the hot jars, then pack the cucumbers in tightly. Pour the warm vinegar mixture into the warm jars, leaving a 1 cm (½ inch) gap at the top of each jar. Both the liquid and the jars need to be warm to ensure that the lids seal properly. Also, make sure the cucumbers are completely submerged; if they aren't, you can lay one cucumber baton or slice flat across the top, to push them down. Tap gently to make sure there are no air bubbles.

Using paper towel, wipe the rims clean. Screw the lids on and leave until cool.

Leave for 2 weeks before eating, or store for up to 6 months. Once opened, store in the fridge.

When made from scratch, ginger pickles have a beautiful soft pink blush, which is worlds away from the glowing technicoloured preservative-laden stuff you'll find in most sushi joints. The pink colour occurs naturally when you use very young ginger. Harvested in summer, young ginger has thin skin with touches of pink. Look for it in your Asian grocery store or good greengrocer. If you can't find it, or it's the wrong season, don't let that stop you. Made with older ginger, which is a little more fibrous, your pickles will be a pretty pale yellow and will have a stronger ginger taste.

PICKLED GINGER

MAKES: 1 x 280 ml (10 oz) jar

METHOD

Wash a small glass jar in very hot soapy water, then rinse well and place on a tea towel to air dry. There is no need to properly sterilise the jar, as this pickle will be kept in the fridge.

Gently heat the vinegar, salt and sugar in a small saucepan and stir until the sugar has dissolved. Remove from the heat and leave to cool slightly.

While the syrup is cooling, peel the papery skin off the ginger by either scraping it with a teaspoon, or using a small sharp knife. Slice into very thin rounds with a vegetable peeler or mandoline. You should end up with about 1 cup.

Pack the sliced ginger tightly into your jar and cover with the warm vinegar mixture; you may have some brine left over. Clean the rim of your jar with paper towel and screw the lid on.

Leave to cool, then store in the fridge for at least 24 hours before using. The pickled ginger will keep for about 2 months.

INGREDIENTS

250 ml (9 fl oz/1 cup) rice wine vinegar
1 teaspoon sea salt
55 g (2 oz/¼ cup) raw or granulated
   white sugar
15 cm (6 inch) knob of fresh
   young ginger

HOW TO USE

- Serve alongside your favourite sushi.
- Use the brine instead of vinegar in salad dressings, for a gentle hit of ginger.
- Pour any leftover brine over peeled and thinly sliced carrots, leave to marinate for 30 minutes, then use on a baguette with chicken, pâté and coriander (cilantro) for a Vietnamese-style roll.

Clockwise from top left: Farmers' market pickles (page 71);
Quick cucumber pickles (page 76); Pickled ginger (page 77);
Bread & butter pickles (page 74); Sweet mustard pickles (page 75).

CHUTNEY

Chutneys are a great project for beginners. You basically throw everything in the pot and it simmers away to create a luscious, thick, jammy sauce. You'll know when chutney is ready because it will be a lovely deep colour, and will part like the Red Sea when you pull a wooden spoon through it. If you taste it as soon as you make it and think it is a little too hot or too vinegary, be patient: the trick with chutney is to let it sit for at least a few weeks before you use it, so the flavours can mellow and get to know each other a little.

With the chutneys in this book, if any of the jars don't seal properly (see Jam 101, page 55), store the jar in the fridge and use within 1 month.

MAKES: 4 x 280 ml (10 oz) jars
(depending on how large and juicy your fruit is)

INGREDIENTS

1 kg (2 lb 4 oz) peaches or nectarines,
   or a mix of both
1 red capsicum (pepper)
1 small onion
1 red chilli
5 cm (2 inch) knob of fresh ginger
4 garlic cloves
125 ml (4 fl oz/½ cup) apple
   cider vinegar
150 g (5½ oz/¾ cup, lightly packed)
   brown sugar
60 g (2¼ oz/⅓ cup) raisins
1 teaspoon sea salt

EQUIPMENT

4 x 280 ml (10 oz) jars and lids
sharp knife
large heavy-based saucepan
wooden spoon
ladle
paper towel

CHUTNEY METHOD

《(1)

Prepare your jars: Sterilise your jars using a method outlined on page 55. Keep them warm until you are ready to use them.

Chop the fruit and vegetables: Remove the stones from the fruit and chop the flesh into bite-sized pieces. Finely dice the capsicum, onion and chilli. Peel the ginger by scraping off the papery skin with a teaspoon or small sharp knife, then grate. Peel and chop the garlic.

(2)》

Combine: Put the vinegar and sugar in a large heavy-based saucepan. Stir in the chopped fruit, capsicum, onion, chilli, ginger, garlic, raisins and salt, then bring to the boil.

Simmer: Reduce the heat and simmer for 20–30 minutes. If the peaches are still firm, cook for several minutes more until they become very soft. The chutney is ready when it holds its shape when you move a wooden spoon through it; if any liquid runs in behind the spoon, keep cooking for a few more minutes.

Remove and cool: Remove from the heat and allow to cool slightly.

Bottle, seal and store: Ladle the warm chutney carefully into warm jars, leaving a 1 cm (½ inch) gap at the top of each jar. Wipe the rims clean with paper towel, screw the lids on and leave to cool. Store for about 1–2 weeks before using, as the chutney needs some time to mellow. Once cooled, it will keep for up to 6 months.

HOW TO USE

- Grab some rye bread, add a good slather of chutney and pile high with ham, vintage cheddar cheese and fresh herbs.
- Great on a cheese platter with sharp cheeses such as Manchego.
- Fold through one of the Sausage mixes on pages 201–204 for a meatloaf with extra flavour.
- Perfect with rich meats like pulled pork sandwiches.

My brother Benjamin considers himself a pretty good cook, and he isn't wrong. This is his winter chutney, which we've started making each year as soon as pears and apples hit the markets. This is a robust chutney: dark brown like molasses, slightly sweet, but with a gentle chilli kick. It is perfect with the sausages on page 201, on a hamburger instead of tomato sauce, or folded through couscous to go with a root vegetable tagine. Or you can double the chilli and serve it with your favourite Indian curry.

BEN'S WINTER CHUTNEY

MAKES: 3 x 280 ml (10 oz) jars

INGREDIENTS

1 kg (2 lb 4 oz) mixed cooking apples and pears
½ lemon
1 red capsicum (pepper)
2 brown onions
2 garlic cloves, peeled
375 ml (13 fl oz/1½ cups) apple cider vinegar
285 g (10 oz/1½ cups, lightly packed) brown sugar
170 g (6 oz/1 cup) raisins
1 fresh or dried bay leaf
2 teaspoons chilli flakes, or 1 fresh chilli, seeded and finely chopped
1 tablespoon black mustard seeds
1 cinnamon stick
1 tablespoon ground ginger
3 cloves

METHOD

Sterilise your jars and lids using a method outlined on page 55. Keep them warm until you are ready to use them.

Peel, core and roughly chop the apples and pears. Chop the lemon, including the peel, and discarding the seeds.

Roughly chop the capsicum, onions and garlic.

Add all the ingredients, including the spices, to a large heavy-based saucepan and gently bring to the boil. Reduce the heat and simmer for 1–1½ hours, or until the apple and pear have broken down and the chutney is dark brown. The chutney is ready when it holds its shape when you move a wooden spoon through it; if any liquid runs in behind the spoon, keep cooking for a few more minutes.

Remove from the heat and allow to cool in the pan for 15 minutes. Ladle carefully into warm jars, leaving a 1 cm (½ inch) gap at the top of each jar. Wipe the rims clean with paper towel, screw the lids on and leave to cool.

Leave for about 1–2 weeks before using, for the flavours to mellow. The chutney will keep in the pantry for up to 6 months. Once opened, store in the fridge.

Make this with ripe tomatoes at the height of summer and you'll have a bright red relish to use for the rest of the year. Adapted from an old recipe that can be found in country cookbooks from the 1930s, it is mysteriously named after a city in what is now known as Pakistan.

TOMATO QUETTA

MAKES: 4 x 500 ml (16 oz) jars

METHOD

Sterilise your jars and lids using a method outlined on page 55. Keep them warm until you are ready to use them.

Bring a large saucepan of water to the boil. Using a small sharp knife, make a cross on the base of each tomato and place in the boiling water for 1 minute. When you see the skin starting to peel away from the cross, remove the tomatoes from the boiling water. Leave to cool, then peel the skin away.

Using your hands, crush the tomatoes into a medium heavy-based saucepan. Add the remaining ingredients, except the flour.

Bring to the boil over high heat, then reduce to a simmer and leave to bubble away for up to 45 minutes, or until the mixture is thick. At this point, remove a small amount of the tomato mixture with a cup and add the flour. Blend to a smooth, runny paste, then stir back into the chutney.

Carefully ladle the chutney into the warm jars, leaving a 1 cm (½ inch) gap at the top of each jar. Using paper towel, clean the rims of the jars, then screw the lids on and leave until cool.

Eat straight away, or store in the pantry for up to 6 months. Once opened, store in the fridge.

INGREDIENTS

2.5 kg (5 lb 8 oz) ripe tomatoes
4 garlic cloves, crushed
5 cm (2 inch) knob of fresh ginger, peeled and grated (about 30 g/ 1 oz grated ginger)
1 small red chilli, chopped (keeping the seeds if you want extra heat)
330 g (11½ oz/1½ cups) raw sugar
100 g (3½ oz) sultanas (golden raisins)
250 ml (9 fl oz/1 cup) apple cider vinegar
2 tablespoons sea salt flakes
2 tablespoons plain (all-purpose) flour

People hold strong opinions about what makes the perfect burger. Here are my rules. Firstly, start with really good meat that is well seasoned; use any one of the sausage mixes listed on pages 201–204, or simply use a cut such as chuck steak, with a fat content of around 20 per cent. Always use good-quality condiments – a home-made chutney, or the Tomato Quetta on page 85 – and good cheese. And finally, two tips for cooking: make an indent with your thumb in the middle of the patty so it cooks evenly, and weigh each patty so they all take the same time to cook. Follow these simple rules and you'll be on your way!

THE BEST EVER BURGER

SERVES 4

INGREDIENTS

400 g (14 oz) sausage mixture
    (from one of the sausage recipes
    on pages 201–204)
1 tablespoon vegetable oil
4 slices of sharp cheddar cheese
4 brioche buns, or your favourite
    bread rolls
butter, for spreading
200 g (7 oz/⅔ cup) Chutney (page 80)
4 slices of tomato (if in season)
4 inner leaves of an iceberg lettuce
    or in-season salad greens
1 small red onion, thinly sliced
    into rings

METHOD

Put the sausage mixture in a bowl. Make sure it is well combined by mixing with your hands for a good 2 minutes; it should be sticky.

Divide the sausage mixture into four even portions, then shape into patties about 3 cm (1¼ inches) high. Put an indent in the top with your thumb to help them cook evenly.

Heat a large heavy-based frying pan until screamingly hot. Add the vegetable oil, swirl it around the pan, then add your patties. Cook over high heat for 3 minutes, then reduce the heat to medium. Flip them over, top each with a slice of cheese and cook for a further 3 minutes. Remove from the pan and leave to rest for 2 minutes while you get the buns ready.

Split the buns in half and lightly toast them under a hot grill (broiler), cut side up. Slather the cut sides with butter and chutney.

Layer the bottom buns with the tomato and lettuce. Top with the patties, then the onion and another dollop of chutney. Pop on the tops and there you have it!

CHAPTER THREE
DAIRY

BUTTER

I first made butter by putting a litre of good organic cream and a few marbles in a jar and spending 10 minutes enthusiastically shaking it, proving you don't need fancy equipment and a country farmhouse to indulge in cooking from scratch. Seeing cream turn into a mass of glossy yellow butter surrounded by a puddle of buttermilk is the most magical process, and I really recommend having a go. When you try it, you'll be delighted with a taste that is worlds away from the store-bought stuff, and you'll be even more pleased because it takes nearly zero kitchen skills to prepare.

However, your butter will only be as good as your cream, so seek out the best organic cream you can find and make a big batch, then freeze some of your butter for later. You also end up with a good amount of buttermilk, which you should never throw away, as it gives a wonderful tang to cakes, cornbread and pancakes.

MAKES: 285 g (10 oz) butter, plus 650 ml (22½ fl oz) buttermilk

INGREDIENTS

1 litre (35 fl oz/4 cups) good-quality
organic thin (pouring) cream

EQUIPMENT

electric stand mixer, with whisk attachment
and bowl
tea towel
colander lined with muslin (cheesecloth)
large bowl
airtight container for the buttermilk
baking paper

BUTTER METHOD

« ① **Get your mixer ready:** Fit your electric stand mixer with the whisk attachment.

Start mixing: Pour the cream into the mixer bowl. Start the mixer on medium–high speed. At this point I like to drape a damp tea towel over the mixer, to stop splatters of cream redecorating the kitchen.

② **»**

Keep mixing: After 2½ minutes of mixing, the cream will start going through four stages. First it will thicken into stiff whipped cream; you can remove the tea towel at this point.

After about 5 minutes, the cream will begin to turn yellow.

After a few more minutes, the cream will begin to split, and buttermilk will start swishing around the bottom of the bowl; the butter will resemble popcorn.

Keep beating for a few more minutes, until the butter and the buttermilk become separated.

 Drain the buttermilk: Set your muslin-lined colander over a large bowl. Pour the butter mixture into the colander, so the buttermilk drains into the bowl below.

4 »

Squeeze out the liquid: Draw up the sides of the muslin and give the butter a good squeeze to release the buttermilk. Transfer the buttermilk to an airtight container; it will keep for 1 week in the fridge, or can be frozen for later use.

« 5

Rinse, knead and wrap: Rinse the butter in cold water, then knead to release more buttermilk. Rinse again and knead for a few more seconds to release as much buttermilk as possible; if too much buttermilk remains, the butter will go rancid. When no more buttermilk is released, add sea salt to taste, or your favourite herbs or spices. Wrap the butter in baking paper. Store in the fridge, where it will keep for up to 3 months, or freeze for up to 6 months.

HOW TO USE

- Mix some finely chopped fresh oregano, rosemary, garlic or dill through your butter, and use on everything from grilled scallops to barbecued steaks.
- Make an amazing seaweed butter. Melt the butter slowly in a small saucepan. When nearly golden, add a sheet of shredded nori, then blend with a hand-held blender until smooth. When cool, serve with steamed fish and a side of greens.
- Make a decadent butter icing for your favourite cake.
- Use the buttermilk for making Cornbread (page 123), as a substitute for milk in cakes and pancakes, or to make buttermilk fried chicken.

YOGHURT

After spending years mucking around with all manner of methods for making yoghurt, I've finally found the perfect recipe to create delicious thick yoghurt every time, based on a method from fermentation guru Sandor Katz. It rests on two key processes: simmering the milk to ensure a thicker yoghurt, and housing the yoghurt in an Esky or portable cooler, providing a warm, stable environment while it does its thing.

This recipe is very simple, but for it to work you do need the best ingredients, starting with good-quality organic unhomogenised milk. Homogenisation is a mechanical process that disperses all the fat globules throughout the milk, so the cream doesn't form a layer on top; in my book, cream is good! You'll also need some yoghurt to use as your starter culture.

This is a perfect project for little people. My little one eats a ton of it every week! Making it from scratch is cheaper for me, and she loves being part of the process.

MAKES: 2 x 500 ml (16 oz) jars

INGREDIENTS

500 ml (17 fl oz/2 cups) boiling water
1 litre (35 fl oz/4 cups) unhomogenised
    full-cream milk, preferably organic;
    the better the milk, the better your
    yoghurt will be
1 tablespoon plain store-bought
    yoghurt, at room temperature,
    as your starter culture

EQUIPMENT

Esky or portable cooler
medium heavy-based saucepan
    or double boiler
cooking thermometer
wooden spoon
small bowl
2 x 500 ml (16 oz) jars with lids,
    sterilised using a method on page 55
paper towel

YOGHURT METHOD

1 **Prepare your Esky:** Pour the 500 ml (17 fl oz/2 cups) boiling water into an Esky or portable cooler. After 15 minutes, empty the water out and close the lid to retain the heat.

2 »

Warm the milk: In a medium heavy-based saucepan or double boiler, very slowly and gently heat the milk to 82°C (180°F). It should not be boiling, but lightly foaming around the edges. Keep your milk at this temperature for 10 minutes, over very low heat. Watch it like a hawk and stir every now and then with a wooden spoon, so it doesn't catch on the bottom of the pan.

3 **Cool the milk:** Take the milk off the heat and leave to cool to 46°C (115°F). If you want to speed this bit up, sit the pan in a sink full of cold water to hurry things along.

« **4**

Mix the milk and starter culture: When the milk has cooled to 46°C (115°F), pour 125 ml (4 fl oz/½ cup) into a small bowl, then mix in your tablespoon of yoghurt, making sure there are no lumps. Now stir this mixture back into the rest of the milk.

 (5) **Fill your jars:** Pour the mixture into your jars; wipe the rims clean using paper towel. Screw the lids on.

(6) **»**

Leave to ferment:
Place the jars in your warmed Esky, close the lid and leave overnight.

 (7)

Tuck in: After 8–12 hours, the jars should be full of yoghurt; if you are lucky there will be a layer of cream on top. Transfer your yoghurt to the fridge and use within 1 week. You can use this yoghurt as your starter for your next batch, but it will only last for another three to five more batches. After this, start again with 1 tablespoon of store-bought yoghurt.

HOW TO USE

- Blend with strawberries and peaches and freeze for an instant summer sorbet.
- Tenderise meat with a mix of yoghurt, garlic, ginger, olive oil, cumin and lemon juice before barbecuing.
- Make some creamy Labne (page 98).
- For a great sauce for lamb chops, mash with sharp feta cheese, salt, lemon juice and fresh herbs.

LABNE

Here is your fail-safe introduction to making cheese. Beautifully thick and creamy, labne is actually more a strained yoghurt rather than a cheese. It is delicious, slightly tart and a cinch to make. It needs time to strain, so start preparing it the day before you'd like to use it. Try mixing some finely chopped fresh rosemary, oregano or a small amount of garlic through your labne and serving it with home-made Crackers (page 133) or flatbread.

MAKES: 500 g (1 lb 2 oz), approximately

INGREDIENTS

1 teaspoon sea salt
1 kg (2 lb 4 oz) Greek-style yoghurt;
   (the thickness of your yoghurt, and
   how long you strain it, will determine
   how much labne you end up with)

EQUIPMENT

sieve or colander
large bowl
muslin (cheesecloth)
spoon

LABNE METHOD

(1) **Prepare your bowl:** Place a sieve or colander over a large bowl and line it with muslin (cheesecloth). Double the muslin over so you have two layers.

Get your yoghurt ready: Stir the salt through the yoghurt.

(2)

Place in the bowl: Scoop the yoghurt into the middle of the muslin-lined sieve.

 (3)

Tie up like a parcel: Gather the edges of the cloth, pull them together and tie them into a knot, to form a parcel. It should look like a Christmas pudding.

Drain: Keeping the sieve resting over the bowl to catch the drips, place the whole thing in the fridge and leave to drain. Leave for 12 hours for a soft cheese, or 24 hours for a firm labne.

Strain, squeeze and eat: When your labne is the texture you'd like it to be, gently squeeze out the excess liquid, then remove from the cloth. Serve fresh, or try the serving suggestions below. The labne will keep in an airtight container in the fridge for up to 1 week.

HOW TO USE

- Fold the juice and finely grated zest of 1 lemon through. Serve on Crackers (page 133), with Gravlax (page 195) or grilled fish.
- Perfect with grilled asparagus and fresh herbs for a simple salad.
- Omit the salt, whisk through some sugar and lemon juice and serve with seasonal fruits and fresh mint.
- Pile a chickpea burger with fresh sliced tomato, coriander (cilantro) leaves and a thick spread of labne.

This is such an easy recipe and always impressive. To shape the balls of labne, either use two spoons to form them into quenelles, or simply use slightly damp hands. Flavour the oil with whatever is in season – fresh bay leaves, oregano, chillies… The labne balls can be used on a meze plate with home-made Crackers (page 133) and Gravlax (page 195), strewn across a salad of fresh heirloom tomatoes and basil in summer, or in the cooler months tossed with radicchio leaves, baked mushrooms and thyme. When you've used up all your marinated labne, don't throw the oil away, as it makes a delicious addition to dressings or grilled vegetables and meats.

MARINATED LABNE

MAKES: 2 x 500 ml (16 oz) jars

METHOD

Sterilise your jars and lids, using a method outlined on page 55.

Divide the herbs and chilli between the jars, then fill each jar with both the oils. (Don't be tempted to use only olive oil, as it will harden in the fridge.)

Using two spoons, or your hands, roll the labne into balls and drop them into the oil. Repeat until the jars are full.

Screw the lids on and store in the refrigerator. The labne will keep for up to 2 weeks.

INGREDIENTS

4 tablespoons chopped fresh herbs
    such as rosemary, oregano
    and thyme
1 long mild red chilli, cut in
    half lengthways
250 ml (9 fl oz/1 cup) olive oil,
    approximately
250 ml (9 fl oz/1 cup) light-tasting
    vegetable oil, such as canola
500 g (1 lb 2 oz) firm Labne (page 98)

CHEAT'S RICOTTA

One of my great joys is watching milk transform into soft, creamy curds. This recipe is cheese-making at its simplest, and something everyone should try at least once – not only because it works out cheaper than buying it from the deli, but it is also really easy.

This cheese is not technically a ricotta, which is made from whey, but is similar in texture. Make sure you fork out the extra money to get the best organic, full-cream unhomogenised milk you can find – it makes all the difference. And never use skim milk, as it doesn't have the requisite amount of cream for the curds to form nicely.

Spoon your fresh curds onto a thick piece of good bread, top with tomato, basil, a sprinkle of sea salt and a drizzle of good olive oil, and you have perfection.

MAKES: 450 g (1 lb/2 cups)

INGREDIENTS

2 litres (70 fl oz/8 cups) organic, unhomogenised full-cream milk
125 ml (4 fl oz/½ cup) thin (pouring) cream
1 teaspoon sea salt
2 tablespoons lemon juice

EQUIPMENT

medium heavy-based saucepan
sugar thermometer
slotted spoon
fine-meshed sieve or colander, double-lined with muslin (cheesecloth) and set over a bowl
jug for storing the whey
bowl for storing the ricotta

CHEAT'S RICOTTA METHOD

 《①

Combine the ingredients: In a medium heavy-based saucepan, combine the milk, cream and salt.

Bring to the boil: Slowly bring the milk to a gentle simmer, or until it registers 85°C (185°F) on a sugar thermometer; the milk should be frothy around the edges, with a few bubbles in the middle. Add the lemon juice.

②**》**

Leave for 2 minutes: Reduce the heat and keep cooking at a slow simmer for a few minutes, until you start to see the milk separating. You'll notice some little soft white lumps floating around. Don't be tempted to stir it now, or you'll break the curds.

Take off the heat and leave: When the whey is turning yellow and the curds are nice and thick, take the pan off the heat. Leave for 30 minutes, so the curds can develop some more.

≪ ③

Drain: Using a slotted spoon, transfer the curds to a colander lined with muslin, set over a bowl. Leave to drain for about 1 hour. Keep the whey that collects in the bowl to use in making breads, or wherever water is called for in baking. The whey will keep for up to 1 week in the fridge, or can be frozen for later use.

Eat: Once drained, transfer to an airtight container, or place in a bowl and cover with plastic wrap, then store in the fridge, where it will firm up a little. You can also put it into a mould at this point and drain for a further day or two for a firmer cheese.

HOW TO USE

- Gently stir finely chopped basil, oregano and thyme through the curds and serve as a dip with home-made Crackers (page 133).
- Stir through pasta with roasted zucchini (courgette) and plenty of basil and parmesan cheese.
- Use the leftover whey in baking breads or cakes, or for braising or slow-cooking meats.

I've been making this appetiser (or, as some fancy people say, hors d'oeuvre) forever, for the simple reason that it's so easy to make, but is also rather sophisticated, which suits me to a tee. The unexpected combination of honey and black pepper with the soft ricotta is delicious. The sprinkle of thyme is optional, but in my opinion makes it nearly perfect. The secret to this dish is to have the best quality ingredients on hand. Choose a strong tasting local raw honey, freshly ground black pepper and very fresh ricotta. The bread must be a good chewy sourdough and when you toast or grill it, don't be scared to char it a little. It adds to the flavour. Serve with a cold, dry white wine.

RICOTTA, HONEY & THYME CROSTINI

SERVES 8

INGREDIENTS

8 slices No-knead Bread (page 118)
    or sourdough
2 tablespoons olive oil
250 g (9 oz) Cheat's ricotta (page 104)
2 tablespoons honey
thyme sprigs, to garnish

METHOD

Brush each piece of bread lightly with olive oil, and toast under a hot grill (broiler) on both sides.

Once the toast has cooled slightly, spread each piece with the ricotta, then drizzle with honey and add a good grinding of black pepper.

Garnish with thyme sprigs and serve.

This is a beautiful way to eat ricotta. You'll be amazed at how the creamy ricotta curds transform into a smooth, silky sauce with a few turns of a whisk. The vanilla and sugar make it even more delicious, but feel free to add some maple syrup or honey instead.

The chocolate sauce is also magic. If you have any left over, use it on top of ice cream, where it will quickly harden, and you'll need to whack it with the back of a spoon before you tuck in.

POACHED PEARS WITH WHIPPED RICOTTA & CHOCOLATE SAUCE

SERVES 4

METHOD

Place the ricotta, icing sugar and vanilla in a small bowl. Using a whisk, mix until smooth and silky.

In a small saucepan, melt the coconut oil and the chocolate over low heat, stirring with a wooden spoon until the mixture is melted and shiny.

Place the preserved pears in shallow serving bowls and drizzle each with a tablespoon of their preserving syrup. Add a big dollop of whipped ricotta, then drizzle with the chocolate sauce. Garnish with star anise and cinnamon sticks, if desired.

INGREDIENTS

460 g (1 lb/2 cups) Cheat's ricotta (page 104)
2 tablespoons icing (confectioners') sugar
½ teaspoon natural vanilla extract, or the seeds from ½ vanilla bean
65 g (2½ oz/⅔ cup) coconut oil
150 g (5½ oz/1 cup) chopped good-quality dark chocolate
4 Preserved pears (page 41)
star anise, to garnish (optional)
cinnamon sticks, to garnish (optional)

MILK KEFIR

All food has a story, and this is one of my favourites. In 1979, the parents of a mate of mine were preparing to leave Russia, and her mother couldn't bear the thought of not being able to take her kefir grains with her – making kefir was a daily ritual in her kitchen, as in many other Russian households. She secretly smuggled her precious kefir grains under the noses of multiple customs officers until they landed safely in Australia. Over 30 years later, the grains are still producing delicious milk kefir, not just for their family but mine and many others.

An ancient drink, milk kefir (pronounced kee-fir) is the most popular fermented milk drink in many parts of Eastern Europe, and is quite similar to yoghurt, but contains many more beneficial probiotics, so is even better for you! It is very simple to make and is perfect in smoothies, on muesli or as cream cheese; you can also add it to your sourdoughs, or use as a substitute for buttermilk in baking. You can find milk kefir in some supermarket dairy cabinets, but often these are pasteurised, so it is best to make it yourself.

As with Water kefir (page 164), you'll need some milk kefir 'grains' to help the milk ferment. Small and jelly-like, these are similar in shape to cauliflower florets, but are not actually grains at all. You can buy them online and at good health food shops … or steal some from a Russian friend's mum.

MAKES: 300–500 ml (10½–17 fl oz)

INGREDIENTS

500 ml (17 fl oz/2 cups) organic, unhomogenised full-cream milk
1 tablespoon milk kefir grains

EQUIPMENT

1 x 600 ml (21 oz) jar, and a small cloth to cover the top of the jar
rubber band for securing the cloth
small fine-mesh strainer
1 x 500 ml (16 oz) jar with a lid, to store your finished kefir in the fridge

MILK KEFIR METHOD

 Prepare your jar: Wash a 600 ml (21 oz) jar with hot soapy water, place on a clean tea towel and leave to air dry.

Fill: Pour the milk into your jar and add your milk kefir grains.

Leave to brew: Loosely cover the jar with a cloth and secure with a rubber band. Leave on the kitchen bench, or in a warm spot out of direct sunlight. After about 12 hours the milk will start to separate and begin to smell a little funky; this is okay and is meant to happen.

Strain: After about 24 hours, the milk will have separated some more, and will smell both sweet and a little sour. This is what you want. Strain the kefir through a small strainer, into your clean 500 ml (16 oz) jar, reserving the kefir grains. Give the strained kefir a good stir.

Reserve the grains: Return the reserved kefir grains to the original jar and cover with 125 ml (4 fl oz/½ cup) of the strained kefir. Place in the fridge; the grains will keep for several weeks.

Drink: Seal your jar of fresh milk kefir and store in the fridge. Use within 1 week.

Prepare the next batch: Bring the reserved kefir grains and kefir milk back to room temperature. Add 375 ml (13 fl oz/1½ cups) fresh unhomogenised full-cream milk and follow the process again.

HOW TO USE

- Use in place of yoghurt in a summery peach and vanilla smoothie.
- Add to granola and stewed fruit for breakfast.
- Use in place of buttermilk when baking cornbread or cakes.
- Swirl through your favourite winter soup to add a creamy tang.

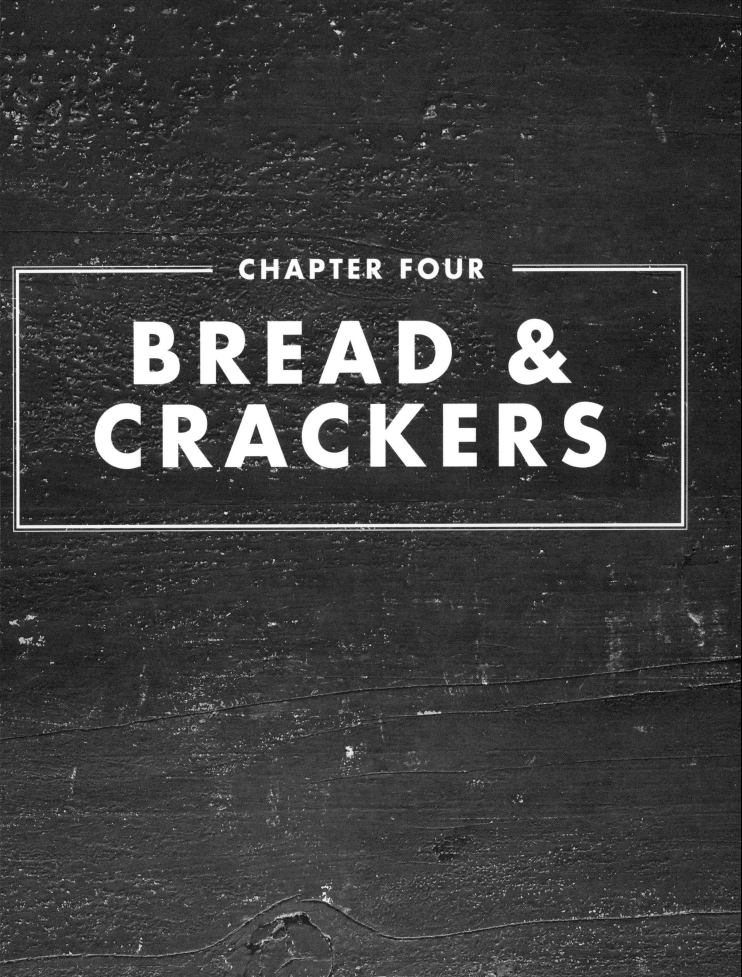

CHAPTER FOUR

BREAD & CRACKERS

NO-KNEAD BREAD

This is the bread that really got me into bread-making. Based on the recipe made famous by Jim Lahey at Sullivan St Bakery, it cannot be any simpler – no special ingredients or skills required. Just a little time, as it takes around 24 hours to make. And a heavy pot with a lid; cast iron works best.

Once you've mastered this, store-bought bread will be a thing of the past. Don't be tempted to add more yeast to the dough, as the long fermentation time is what makes the dough rise. When you have the process down pat, you can start experimenting with different flours, and add some nuts, seeds or spices. I'm a fan of walnuts and dates, with a little bit of spelt flour to add some extra body.

The most important tip for all bread-making is to not tuck in straight away once you've pulled the loaf out of the oven. I understand the temptation to crack open a hot loaf of bread and slather it with butter while admiring your handiwork. But at this exact moment, the loaf is still cooking, so leave it for 30 minutes at least, so it can continue to do its thing. If you have the patience, you'll thank me.

MAKES: 1 loaf

INGREDIENTS

300 g (10½ oz/2 cups) strong white
　　flour (also called 'bread flour'),
　　plus extra for dusting
150 g (5½ oz/1 cup) plain wholemeal
　　(whole-wheat) flour
¼ teaspoon active dried yeast
1 teaspoon sea salt
375 ml (13 fl oz/1½ cups)
　　lukewarm water

EQUIPMENT

large bowl
large mixing spoon
plastic wrap
40 cm (16 inch) square of baking paper
cast-iron saucepan with a lid
oven mitts
wire cooling rack

NO-KNEAD BREAD METHOD

(1) »

Mix dry ingredients: In a large bowl, mix the flours, yeast and salt so they are combined.

Add water and stir: Pour in the lukewarm water and stir well with a large spoon. The mixture will be shaggy, sticky and a little on the wet side. This is totally normal and what you want.

Cover and leave: Cover the bowl with plastic wrap and leave in a warmish place for 12–18 hours. Yes, this timing is correct and not a misprint – the dough needs a long nap to ferment and rise.

« (2)

Shape and leave again: After 12–18 hours, the dough will have bubbles on top and will have doubled in size. Tip the dough out onto a floured work bench. Quickly fold the edges in towards the middle and shape the bread into a nice round ball. (Don't stress if it isn't perfect – after a few attempts, you'll get a lot more confident with this step and the shape will improve.) Move the dough onto a large piece of baking paper, or into an oiled bowl, seam side down, and leave for another 4 hours.

Preheat the oven and pan: An hour before the bread has finished rising for the second time, preheat the oven to 230°C (450°F) and place your cast-iron pan in the oven, with the lid on, to heat it – a piping-hot pan is one of the secrets to success with this bread.

Put the bread in the oven:
Wearing oven mitts, very carefully
pull the very hot pan out of the oven.
Remove the lid. Slide the bread, still
on the baking paper, into the pan.
(If using a bowl for the second rise
instead of baking paper, simply
transfer the ball of dough into the hot
saucepan with the seam side down.
If it isn't perfect, don't worry. It will
sort itself out in the oven.) Put the lid
on and place in the oven.

Cook: Bake for 30 minutes with
the lid on. Remove the lid and bake
for a further 15 minutes, to give the
bread a lovely golden crust.

Remove and cool: Take the
bread out of the oven and transfer
from the pan to a cooling rack.
Give the bottom of the loaf a tap:
if it is ready, it will sound hollow.
If it doesn't sound hollow, simply
bake for a further 5–10 minutes.
Resist the temptation to eat the bread
immediately. Leave the loaf for a
good 30 minutes, so it can cook
right through.

HOW TO USE

- Try different flours, including rye and spelt, to give the loaf a heavier texture.
- Sweeten it up by adding dried fruits such as figs, dates or currants.
- Replace half the water with your favourite beer to give an earthier flavour.
- Spices work beautifully. Try cinnamon with dates, or cardamom with figs.

CORNBREAD

I'm totally addicted to cornbread. Both savoury and a little sweet, the original recipe was given to me by my friend Ben Meyer, a fantastic chef in Oregon, whose grandmother gave it to him… so you know it must be good!

Unlike wheat bread, which requires plenty of time and patience, this bread will take you 5 minutes to make and will be on the table within the hour. It has become my go-to when I run out of bread and need a quick fix that is nearly impossible to ruin.

To make it a little fancy, you can add some dried smoked chilli or cooked corn kernels; you can also reduce the sugar slightly, but remember that real cornbread is meant to be a little sweet.

Serve alongside a Southern US–inspired dinner of fried chicken, or spicy pulled pork with steamed green beans and your favourite local beer. It's also great slathered with fresh butter and honey for breakfast.

MAKES: 1 loaf, serving up to 6 people

INGREDIENTS

125 g (4½ oz) butter
250 ml (9 fl oz/1 cup) buttermilk,
    or 185 ml (6 fl oz/¾ cup) milk and
    70 g (2½ oz/¼ cup) plain yoghurt
1 free-range egg
180 g (6 oz/1 cup) cornmeal
    (coarse polenta)
75 g (2½ oz/⅓ cup) granulated white
    sugar, or 2 tablespoons honey
150 g (5½ oz/1 cup) plain
    (all-purpose) flour
½ teaspoon sea salt
½ teaspoon bicarbonate of soda
    (baking soda)
2 finely chopped spring onions (scallions),
    plus extra to serve
sliced long red chilli, to serve (optional)

EQUIPMENT

20 cm (8 inch) square baking tin
    or round cast-iron frying pan
small saucepan
2 bowls
whisk
wooden spoon

CORNBREAD METHOD

(1) **Get your oven ready:** Preheat the oven to 180°C (350°F).

(2) **Prepare your pan:** Using a piece of baking paper (or your fingers), liberally grease your baking tin or frying pan with a teaspoon of the butter.

(3) **Melt and mix your wet ingredients:** Melt the remaining butter in a small saucepan, then remove from the heat and let cool for a few minutes. Whisk the buttermilk and egg in a bowl, then stir in the cooled melted butter.

(4) **Mix your dry ingredients:** In a separate bowl, mix together the cornmeal, sugar, flour, salt, bicarbonate of soda and spring onion until well blended.

(5) **Combine wet and dry:** Pour the wet ingredients into the dry ingredients and stir with a wooden spoon until just combined. Don't have a heavy hand when mixing, as it will make the cornbread tough; it's okay if the batter is a little lumpy.

(6) **Pour and bake:** Pour the batter into the baking tin or frying pan. Bake for 30–35 minutes, or until the top is nicely golden and a toothpick inserted in the centre comes out clean. A few cracks will appear on the surface, which is fine. Serve sprinkled with extra spring onion, and sliced red chilli if desired.

HOW TO USE

- Serve with pulled pork and sautéed seasonal greens for a Southern US–style feast.
- Slather with butter and honey for a decadent breakfast.
- Instead of a loaf, make 6 large muffins for lunchboxes, by baking the batter in a six-hole muffin tin for 20–25 minutes.
- Cut into squares and top with Labne (page 98), Gravlax (page 195) and salmon roe.

PIZZA DOUGH

The promise of a hot, crispy pizza layered with the best the season has to offer – and lots of cheese – is surely the best way to get kids into the kitchen. This pizza dough is a cinch to make, and is one recipe that screams 'family activity'. Per pizza, it also works out seriously cheaper than picking up the phone and calling your local pizza place.

Experiment with seasonal toppings – tomato topped with fresh basil in summer, or mushrooms and mozzarella in winter – and you'll keep everyone happy. See page 130 for some seasonal topping ideas.

MAKES: 2 large or 4 small pizzas

INGREDIENTS

2¼ teaspoons active dried yeast
1 teaspoon granulated white sugar
270 ml (9½ fl oz) warm water
450 g (1 lb/3 cups) plain (all-purpose)
    flour, plus extra for dusting
1 teaspoon sea salt
1 tablespoon extra virgin olive oil,
    plus extra for brushing

EQUIPMENT

small bowl
3–5 larger bowls
pastry brush
plastic wrap
pizza tray lined with baking paper,
    or a pizza stone

PIZZA DOUGH METHOD

(1) »

Activate the yeast: In a small bowl, combine the yeast, sugar and warm water. Set aside for 5 minutes, or until frothy.

Combine everything: In a large bowl, combine the flour and salt, then add the yeast mixture and the olive oil.

« (2)

Knead: Using your hands, bring the mixture together so it forms a loose ball. Turn out onto a lightly floured work bench, dust your hands with some flour and knead for 1–2 minutes, or until the dough is smooth and elastic.

≪ (3)

Leave to rise: Tear the dough into two or four even portions, depending on how many pizzas you want to make. Place in separate bowls that have been brushed with olive oil. Cover with plastic wrap and leave in a warm spot for 1–2 hours, or until the dough balls have doubled in size.

Prepare your oven: Preheat the oven to 240°C (475°F).

(4) ≫

Punch down: After the dough balls have risen, deflate them by punching softly with your fist.

≪ (5)

Roll out and top: On a floured work bench, roll out each dough portion to about 5 mm (¼ inch) thick. Transfer to a pizza tray lined with baking paper, or to a pre-heated pizza stone. Add your toppings (see page 130) and brush the edges of the pizza with olive oil.

Bake and eat: Bake for 7–10 minutes, or until the base is crisp and golden. Serve immediately.

A four-seasons pizza: what could be better? A pizza for every different season, that's what. Once you've made your own pizza dough from scratch (page 127), you don't need heaps of fancy items to top it all off – just a handful of quality ingredients is enough to transform a humble hand-made pizza from simple to sublime.

SEASONAL PIZZAS

MAKES: each variation tops 2 large or 4 small pizzas

SPRING

400 g (14 oz) asparagus spears,
    shaved with a vegetable peeler
50 g (1¾ oz/½ cup) grated
    parmesan cheese
100 g (3½ oz) mozzarella cheese, sliced
8 quail eggs, to crack onto the pizza
    halfway through cooking
extra virgin olive oil, for drizzling over
    the cooked pizzas

SUMMER

125 ml (4½ fl oz/½ cup) Passata
    (page 177)
400 g (14 oz) mozzarella cheese, sliced
2 ripe tomatoes, thinly sliced
sea salt and freshly ground black pepper
extra virgin olive oil, for drizzling over
    the cooked pizzas
basil leaves, for scattering over the
    cooked pizzas
OPTIONAL: anchovies, chilli or olives

AUTUMN

500 g (1 lb 2 oz) pine mushrooms, sliced
    and gently fried in butter and olive oil
400 g (14 oz) taleggio cheese, rind
    removed, chilled and thinly sliced
sprinkling of chopped flat-leaf (Italian) parsley
sea salt and freshly ground black pepper
extra virgin olive oil, for drizzling over
    the cooked pizzas
OPTIONAL: truffle oil

WINTER

extra virgin olive oil, for brushing over
    the pizza bases, and drizzling
    over the cooked pizzas
500 g (1 lb 2 oz) washed potatoes,
    very thinly sliced
2 tablespoons rosemary leaves
sea salt and freshly ground black pepper
OPTIONAL: crushed garlic added to the
    olive oil; a sprinkling of grated
    mozzarella cheese

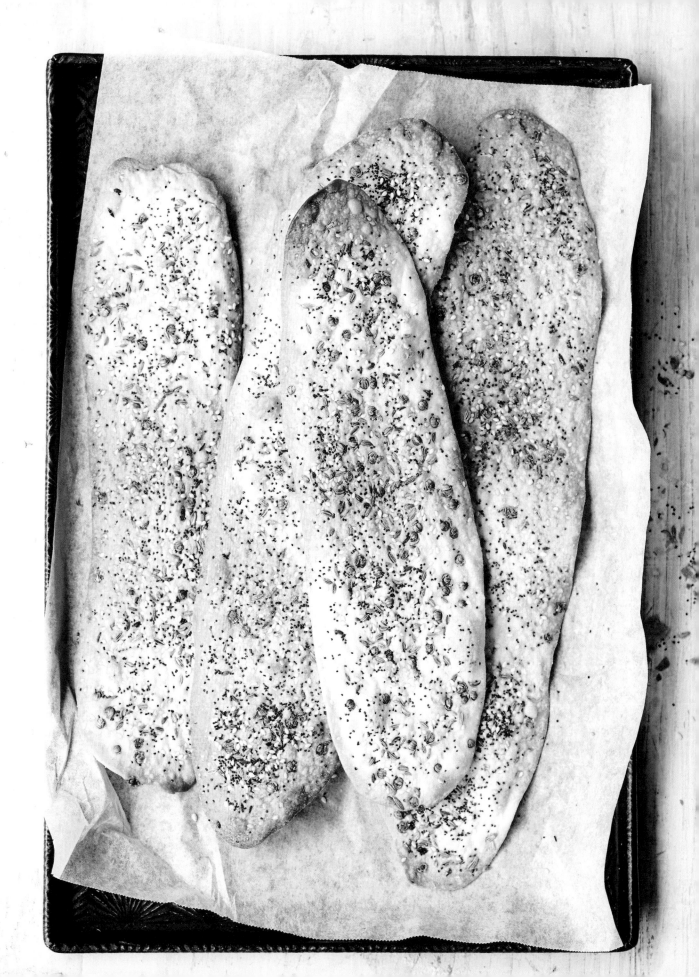

CRACKERS

Walk into any deli and you're almost guaranteed to be gobsmacked by the cost of good crackers. But don't settle for the cheap cardboard-tasting ones from the supermarket – try these instead; they're dead easy to make, the ingredients cost very little, and they taste so amazing you'll never be tempted to buy crackers again.

This is a basic recipe, so feel free to play around with the toppings – smoked salt, different chillies, seeds, dried herbs and spices. Roasting the spices in a small frying pan will really intensify their taste, so please don't skip this step. You can also try incorporating some different flours like spelt and wholemeal (whole-wheat), for extra character and flavour.

The crackers will keep well in an airtight container, so make a double batch and you'll always have some on hand.

MAKES: 8 crackers

INGREDIENTS

1 tablespoon fennel seeds
1 tablespoon poppy seeds
1 tablespoon coriander seeds
1 tablespoon sesame seeds
150 g (5½ oz/1 cup) plain
　　(all-purpose) flour
2 tablespoons olive oil, plus
　　extra for brushing
60 ml (2 fl oz/¼ cup) water,
　　plus 3 teaspoons extra
1 tablespoon sea salt

EQUIPMENT

small frying pan
large mixing bowl
wooden spoon
rolling pin or large bottle
2 baking trays, lined with baking paper
fork
wire cooling rack

CRACKERS METHOD

 Prepare your oven: Preheat the oven to 200°C (400°F).

Dry-fry your spices: In a small frying pan, gently toast the spices over low heat until they are fragrant; this should take about 30 seconds. There is no need to use any oil. This step is important as it brings out the beautiful flavours of the spices.

 Mix your ingredients: In a large bowl, mix the flour, oil and 60 ml (2 fl oz/¼ cup) water, using a wooden spoon, until just combined. The mixture should be a little sticky and shaggy; you may need to add a little extra water, say about 3 teaspoons, depending on the flour and humidity.

 »

Knead the dough: Tip the dough out onto a floured work bench, then knead for about a minute, or until the dough comes together; it should have the texture of a soft playdough. The best thing about this dough is that you can't overwork it. Mixing it only a little will give you a flaky cracker; work it a lot and the crackers will be more uniform in texture.

Roll out: Shape the dough into a log about 30 cm (12 inches long) and cut into eight pieces. Using your rolling pin, roll each piece into an oblong shape that looks like a crocodile's snout. They should be as thin as a piece of paper. If they are too thick, they will be doughy, not crispy. They will also stretch a little more when you transfer them to the baking tray.

Add the toppings: Sprinkle each piece of dough evenly with the salt and the toasted spices. Gently roll the rolling pin over the top to make sure the spices are incorporated, and don't fall off when they are cooked.

Bake: Transfer to baking trays lined with baking paper. Brush with a little olive oil, then prick all over with a fork, to stop air bubbles forming. Bake for 6–8 minutes, or until they are golden.

(6)

Cool and store: Leave to cool on a wire rack. When cooled, transfer to an airtight container and keep in the pantry. The crackers are best consumed within 2 weeks.

HOW TO USE

- Serve with dips such as smoky eggplant (aubergine) dip spiked with pomegranate seeds, or Labne (page 98) drizzled with fruity olive oil.
- Sprinkle with cheese before baking – perfect for little people's lunchboxes.
- For a richer cracker, add a handful of grated cheddar cheese to the dough mixture, and use melted butter instead of olive oil.

This is an unusual yet absolutely delicious way to make an ice cream sandwich. A little lighter than using the traditional biscuits, the crunchy cinnamon crackers are a perfect match with slightly softened vanilla ice cream. Pour yourself an espresso or a shot of your favourite liqueur (old school, I know) and you have a wonderful, albeit messy, way to end a meal.

ICE CREAM CRACKER SANDWICHES

SERVES 4

INGREDIENTS

3 walnut-sized pieces of uncooked Cracker dough (see page 133)
6 tablespoons caster (superfine) sugar, for sprinkling
1 tablespoon ground cinnamon
1 litre (35 fl oz/4 cups) vanilla ice cream

METHOD

Preheat the oven to 200°C (400°F). Line a baking tray with baking paper.

Roll each piece of cracker dough into one long strip, about 30 cm (12 inches) long, as shown on page 134. Sprinkle with the sugar and cinnamon. Gently roll a rolling pin over the top, to crush the sugar into the dough.

Transfer to the baking tray and bake for 6–8 minutes, or until golden. Remove from the oven and leave to cool.

Meanwhile, take the ice cream out of the freezer and leave at room temperature to soften slightly.

Break each cracker into four pieces, each about 7.5 cm (3 inches) long, or to the desired size of your sandwiches. You'll only need eight neat cracker pieces for the four sandwiches, so if all goes perfectly well, you'll end up with more pieces than you need, but some crackers may not break cleanly, so it's handy to have some extra pieces up your sleeve.

Very gently spread a quarter of the softened ice cream on four nice cracker pieces, and top each one with another nice cracker. Serve immediately.

CHAPTER FIVE

FERMENTED FOODS

SAUERKRAUT

If you're interested in fermenting your own vegetables, this is the perfect place to begin. Surprisingly versatile and easy to prepare, sauerkraut is a perfect addition to your kitchen – and making your own rather than buying it from the supermarket yields a much tastier result and is significantly cheaper. I always have a jar of this in the fridge to have on a grilled cheese sandwich, alongside barbecued meats, or to serve with smoked meats and crackers before a meal.

I've detailed a process here, rather than a strict recipe; the only way you'll really learn how to make sauerkraut is to simply get into it. The quantity of ingredients here will make a small batch, so don't fear that you'll have bottle upon bottle of the stuff. A 1 litre (32 oz) jar, or two smaller ones, is perfect to get you started.

Sauerkraut is safe to eat at every stage of the process, so there's no real minimum or maximum fermentation time. Start tasting after a few days, and when you are happy with how it tastes, pop it in the fridge and enjoy. I like it after about a week, but some people leave it for months and love the really funky taste. It's up to you!

MAKES: 1 x 1 litre (32 oz) jar, or 2 x 500 ml (16 oz) jars

INGREDIENTS

1 kg (2 lb 4 oz) cabbage
1 tablespoon sea salt

EQUIPMENT

1 x 1 litre (32 oz) wide-mouthed jar and
        lid, or 2 x 500 ml (16 oz) jars and lids
sharp knife or mandoline
large bowl
rolling pin (optional)

SAUERKRAUT METHOD

(1) »

Clean your jar: Wash your jar (or jars) in hot soapy water and leave to air dry.

Prepare the cabbage: Discard the tough outer leaves of the cabbage. Slice the rest very thinly using a sharp knife or a mandoline; it should look like thin ribbons.

« (2)

Combine the cabbage and salt: This is where you need to get your hands wet and messy. Place the cabbage in a large bowl. Add the salt. Begin crushing the cabbage like you are giving it a good shoulder massage. After about 3 minutes of crunching, liquid will start seeping out of the cabbage, which is what you want. Keep going until the cabbage mixture is dripping with liquid. This can take anywhere up to 10 minutes.

(3) »

Pack into the jar: Pack the cabbage mixture tightly into the jar, pushing down to release any air; the end of a rolling pin works well for this. The cabbage mixture should be covered by its own liquid. A good trick here is to place one of the larger discarded outer leaves of the cabbage on top to keep it submerged. You can also use a smaller jar filled with pebbles, or a small snap-lock bag filled with water.

« (4)

Cover and leave: Place the lid on loosely and leave at room temperature, checking every couple of days, pressing down to make sure the cabbage mixture is submerged in the liquid.

Check in and store: Start tasting at about 3 days, and as soon as you are happy with the balance of sour and sweet, put the jar in the fridge. Once in the fridge, the sauerkraut will last for about 2 months.

HOW TO USE

- Grate a small onion and a few carrots, then mix in a few tablespoons of sauerkraut for a delicious Polish-inspired salad that is perfect with meat.
- Enjoy on a simple grilled cheese sandwich.
- For a nourishing lunch, toss some through cooked brown rice, chickpeas, almonds, sunflower seeds, chopped tomato, cucumber, avocado, coriander (cilantro) and parsley, with a big lug of olive oil and lemon juice.

There are as many different sauerkraut recipes as there are stars in the sky. I usually make a version based on whatever vegetables are in season at the farmers' market, but keeping the basic quantities the same. The variations below are all regulars in my household. The red cabbage and beetroot version goes particularly well with soft cheeses, while the cabbage and fennel sauerkraut is perfect with any cured fish, such as Gravlax (page 195).

RED CABBAGE & CARROT SAUERKRAUT

MAKES: 1 x 1 litre (32 oz) jar, or 2 x 500 ml (16 oz) jars

INGREDIENTS

500 g (1 lb 2 oz) red cabbage
500 g (1 lb 2 oz) carrots,
    thinly sliced
1 tablespoon sea salt
1 teaspoon brown or yellow
    mustard seeds
1 teaspoon fennel seeds

VARIATIONS

CABBAGE & FENNEL
500 g (1 lb 2 oz) green cabbage
500 g (1 lb 2 oz) fennel, including
    a few fronds, thinly sliced
1 tablespoon sea salt
1 teaspoon fennel seeds

RED CABBAGE & BEETROOT
500 g (1 lb 2 oz) red cabbage
500 g (1 lb 2 oz/3½ cups, firmly
    packed) grated fresh beetroot
50 g (1¾ oz/⅓ cup) grated onion
2 tablespoons chopped fresh oregano
2 tablespoons chopped fresh marjoram
2 tablespoons chopped fresh rosemary

METHOD

Wash your jar (or jars) in hot soapy water and leave to air dry.

Remove the tough outer leaves of the cabbage, reserving one large leaf for topping the jar.

Using a sharp knife or a mandoline, slice the rest of the cabbage into thin ribbons and place in a large bowl.

Add the remaining ingredients, then crush them all together with your hands for about 10 minutes, until the mixture is dripping with liquid.

Pack the mixture tightly into your jar, pushing down to release any air; the end of a rolling pin works well for this. The mixture should be covered by its own liquid. Place the reserved outer cabbage leaf on top of the mixture, to keep it all submerged.

Place the lid on loosely and leave at room temperature, checking every couple of days, and pressing down to make sure the vegetable mixture is submerged in the liquid.

Start tasting after about 3 days, and as soon as you are happy with the balance of sour and sweet, put the jar in the fridge. Once in the fridge, the sauerkraut will last for about 2 months.

Clockwise from top right:
Red cabbage & carrot sauerkraut;
Cabbage & beetroot sauerkraut;
Cabbage & fennel sauerkraut.

KIM CHI

This traditional Korean fermented side dish has some seriously devoted fans the world over. A heady mix of spicy and sour, kim chi elevates a simple bowl of rice to a meal with one spoonful. There are hundreds of variations, but this one contains all the essential ingredients. Don't be put off by the funky smell when it is fermenting; traditionally it has been brewed in an outdoor shed or cool underground spot for this very reason. Just be sure to keep it in a well-ventilated spot and you'll be fine.

MAKES: 2 x 1 litre (32 oz) jars

INGREDIENTS

½ large Chinese cabbage, about
    1.5 kg (3 lb 5 oz) in total, cut
    lengthways into thirds, then
    washed and well drained
500 g (1 lb 2 oz) carrots, washed
1 small bunch garlic chives,
    about 75 g (2½ oz) in total
1 large brown onion,
    roughly chopped
1 large sweet red apple,
    cored and chopped
80 ml (2½ fl oz/⅓ cup) fish sauce,
    or 50 g (2¾ oz) sea salt
3 large garlic cloves, peeled
1 tablespoon grated fresh ginger
10 g (¼ oz/½ cup) Korean hot red chilli
    flakes (gochugaru)

EQUIPMENT

2 x 1 litre (32 oz) clean glass jars and
    lids (if there is excess mixture, you
    may need another small jar) – or
    you may prefer to use a jar and lid
    with an airlock
large bowl
blender
spatula
disposable kitchen gloves (optional)
paper towel
2 shallow bowls

KIM CHI METHOD

(1) Prepare your jars: Wash your jars in hot, soapy water, rinse well and leave to air dry.

(2) Chop the vegetables: Chop the cabbage and carrots into bite-sized chunks and place in a large bowl. Cut the garlic chives into 2 cm (¾ inch) lengths and add to the bowl.

(3) Blend remaining ingredients: Put the onion and apple in a blender. Add the fish sauce, garlic, ginger and chilli flakes and blend into a rough paste.

(4) Combine paste and vegetables: Use a spatula to scrape the paste out of the blender, adding it to the chopped vegetables. Rub the paste into the vegetables very firmly for a good minute or two; you may want to wear disposable kitchen gloves while doing this as the chilli flakes are quite hot. The vegetables will slowly start releasing liquid, which is what you want.

(5) Pack your jars: Fill the jars with the mixture, pressing it down firmly to ensure no air or gaps remain and the mixture is immersed in its own liquid. Make sure there is a 5 cm (2 inch) space between the top of the liquid and the lids. Wipe the rims clean with paper towel and screw the lids on.

(6) Leave to ferment: Place each jar in a shallow bowl to catch any juice that may escape. Leave to ferment on your work bench for 4–7 days. The mixture will bubble furiously and then calm down. After 4 days you can open the jars and press the mixture back down in the jar, as it will appear to have grown, due to carbon dioxide being produced by bacteria. It will smell pretty strongly, so keep it in a well-ventilated area. Taste the kim chi regularly during fermentation, to see what you like. I prefer a shorter fermenting time, but others like it really funky.

(7) Store and eat: After 7 days, or when you think the kim chi tastes good, transfer to the fridge, where it will keep for up to 3 months. As you use up the kim chi, you can decant the rest into smaller jars to save space in the fridge.

HOW TO USE

- Spice up your salad dressings with a teaspoon or two of kim chi to add some kick.
- Kim chi and a bowl of fried rice is a match made in heaven.
- Use instead of pickles on a toasted cheese sandwich.
- Enjoy with poached eggs and butter-sautéed kale.

Bibimbap is the ultimate Korean comfort food. Basically it is a big bowl piled high with steaming rice, sesame and soy marinated beef, runny eggs, crisp vegetables, chilli sauce and a good whack of kim chi. It works perfectly. I've used carrots and cucumber here, but you can use whatever vegetables are abundant – mushrooms in autumn, roasted pumpkin in winter, or freshly blanched asparagus in spring. Traditionally you would use the Korean chilli sauce, gochujang, but if you can't find it, substitute your favourite hot chilli sauce.

BIBIMBAP

SERVES 2

INGREDIENTS

200 g (7 oz) beef fillet (rump or topside), thinly sliced
1 tablespoon soy sauce
2 tablespoons sesame oil
200 g (7 oz/1 cup) organic brown rice (either short-grain or long-grain)
2 tablespoons peanut oil
2 free-range eggs
2 garlic cloves, crushed
5 cm (2 inch) knob of fresh ginger, peeled and finely diced
1 carrot, thinly sliced
1 cucumber, sliced
Kim chi (page 147), to serve
1 bunch fresh coriander (cilantro), roots washed and finely chopped, leaves and stems roughly chopped
chilli sauce, to serve

METHOD

Place the beef in a small bowl. Toss with the soy sauce and 1 tablespoon of the sesame oil, then cover and marinate for up to 1 hour.

Wash the rice under cold water to remove any impurities and starch. Cook according to the packet instructions; I like to use the absorption method.

Heat a wok over high heat, until nearly smoking. Add 1 tablespoon of the peanut oil. When it is shimmering, crack the eggs in, then turn the heat down to medium. Fry the eggs until they are crispy on the bottom, but the yolks are still runny. Remove the eggs to a plate.

Heat the remaining peanut oil and sesame oil in the wok. Add the beef, along with the marinade, garlic and ginger. Stir-fry for 1 minute, then remove from the heat.

To assemble the meal, pile two bowls or plates with the cooked rice, beef, carrot and cucumber. Top each with a fried egg, then a good mound of kim chi. Scatter the coriander over and serve immediately, with chilli sauce.

FERMENTED CHILLI SAUCE

This sauce, made by fermenting capsicums (peppers) and hot chillies, has a much more complex flavour than your average chilli sauce. You can make it as hot or mild as you like by adjusting the ratio of chilli and capsicum. Serve it alongside scrambled eggs, chorizo and Cornbread (see page 123) for quite possibly the best hangover cure in the world.

MAKES: 2 x 750 ml (26 oz) jars or bottles

INGREDIENTS

1½ tablespoons sea salt
1 litre (35 fl oz/4 cups) water
5 red capsicums (peppers)
60 ml (2 fl oz/¼ cup) olive oil,
    plus extra for sealing the jar
2 garlic cloves
2 long red chillies
2 tablespoons raw or granulated
    white sugar

EQUIPMENT

large pouring jug
roasting tin
large bowl
plastic wrap
sharp knife
1 x 2 litre (64 oz) jar
food processor or hand-held blender
fine-mesh sieve
2 x 750 ml (26 oz) jars or bottles and
    lids, washed in very hot soapy water,
    then rinsed well and air dried

CHILLI SAUCE METHOD

(1) Make the brine: Put the sea salt and water in a large pouring jug and stir until the salt has dissolved.

(2) Roast the capsicums: Preheat the oven to 200°C (400°F). Place the whole capsicums in a roasting tin, drizzle with the olive oil and toss until coated. Roast for 15–20 minutes, turning after 5 minutes. The skin should be blistered and burnt in places, and the flesh soft to touch. Remove from the oven, place in a large bowl and quickly cover with plastic wrap; this will steam the capsicums and make it easier to remove the skin. Allow to cool, then peel off the blackened skin. Remove the seeds, discarding the liquid in the bowl. Slice the flesh into strips and set aside.

(3) Chop the garlic and chilli: Peel the garlic, smash the cloves with the back of a knife, then roughly chop. Cut the stems off the chillies. The seeds of the chillies are where the heat lives, so remove the seeds if you'd like a milder sauce, or leave them in if you're after some heat. Thinly slice the chillies.

(4) Pack your jar: Add the capsicum, garlic and chilli to your 2 litre (64 oz) jar, then pour in the brine, making sure the capsicums are well covered, but leaving about the top one-quarter of the jar empty, as this mixture will expand as it ferments. There may be some brine left over, which is fine.

(5) Seal and leave: Put the lid on loosely. Accumulating gas will need to escape, so keep an eye on the jar and release the gas by opening the lid every few days. If you have a jar lid with an air lock, this would also work well.

(6) Check in daily: If there is any white mould on top, just skim it off; it isn't harmful. After a few days, the mixture will start bubbling and the liquids and solids will separate. This is normal.

(7) Purée and strain: After a week, purée the capsicum mixture, add the sugar, then strain through a fine-mesh sieve; if you like a chunkier sauce, only lightly purée the capsicum mixture and don't strain it.

(8) Bottle and store: Pour the sauce into two 750 ml (26 fl oz) bottles, then cover with a layer of olive oil to stop mould forming on top. Store your sauce in the fridge, where it will keep for up to 2 months.

After a big night out, this is the breakfast I dream of: silky-soft scrambled eggs, spicy chorizo, salty cornbread and a decent splash of fiery fermented capsicum chilli sauce. It is certain to sort you out.

SPICY EGGS WITH CHORIZO

SERVES 4

METHOD

Heat a large heavy-based frying pan over medium–low heat. Add the olive oil. When the oil is hot, add the chorizo and cook for 8–10 minutes, or until nicely browned and heated through. Remove from the pan, leaving half the chorizo-flavoured oil in the pan, and reserving the remaining chorizo-flavoured oil for serving. Keep warm.

In the same pan, melt the butter over low heat. Whisk the eggs in a large bowl, then add to your pan. Using your wooden spoon, gently push the eggs towards the centre of the pan a few times. This will give you lovely soft scrambled eggs. Don't move the eggs around too much or they will overcook and be tough. When they are three-quarters cooked, remove from the heat and leave for 2 minutes; the residual heat will finish cooking them. Season with sea salt and freshly ground black pepper.

Divide the scrambled eggs among warmed serving plates. Drizzle with the reserved chorizo-flavoured oil. Serve with cornbread, rocket, sliced chilli and your fermented chilli sauce. Great with a Bloody Mary!

INGREDIENTS

2 tablespoons olive oil
2 large or 4 small chorizo sausages, thickly cut on the diagonal
50 g (1¾ oz) butter
12 free-range eggs
Cornbread (page 123), to serve
baby rocket (arugula) leaves, to serve
sliced red chillies, to serve
Fermented chilli sauce (page 153), to serve

KOMBUCHA

Originating in China and Russia, this slightly fermented sweet tea packs a serious probiotic punch and is really delicious. It is not hard to prepare, but it will take you a few times to get used to the process. To make it you need a slightly odd-looking thing called a scoby (a 'symbiotic community of bacteria and yeast'), and this is what will ferment your sweet tea; it is also referred to as a 'mother' culture. You can buy these online, at good food co-ops and health food stores, or from a kombucha-making friend.

There are two stages to making kombucha, and all up it will take you about a week. The first stage will give you a slightly carbonated drink. The second stage is the fun part where you get to flavour the tea however you'd like (see page 163), and make it even fizzier.

MAKES: 1.75 litres (60 fl oz/7 cups)

INGREDIENTS

3 tea bags of black, green or white tea, or any combination of these
500 ml (17 fl oz/2 cups) boiling water, plus 1.5 litres (52 fl oz/6 cups) cool filtered water
220 g (7¾ oz/1 cup) raw or granulated white sugar
1 scoby, also known as a 'mother' culture
125 ml (4 fl oz/½ cup) kombucha tea from a previous batch, or from a store-bought unflavoured, unpasteurised kombucha

EQUIPMENT

small teapot or saucepan
sieve and a bowl for straining
1 x 2 litre (64 oz) glass jar, no lid required
clean tightly woven cloth, for covering the jar
rubber band or kitchen string, for securing the cloth
small jar for storing some kombucha and scobies for your next batch
1 x 1.5 litre (52 fl oz) clean bottle for storing the finished brew

KOMBUCHA METHOD

1 **Make the tea:** Brew the tea in a small teapot or saucepan with the boiling water for about 5 minutes. Add the sugar and stir to dissolve. Strain into your 2 litre (64 oz) brewing jar and add the cool filtered water; the mixture needs to be less than 30°C (86°F) so as not to damage the microbes in the scoby, so leave until completely cool.

Add the culture: Remove your scoby from its 'scoby hotel' (or your previous batch). Add it to the brewing jar, along with your ready-made kombucha tea. The scoby may sink or float in the mix – either is fine. **2 »**

« 3

Cover and leave: Cover the jar with the tightly woven cloth and secure with a rubber band or kitchen string. Place the jar in a spot away from direct sunlight, where the temperature will stay between 20–28°C (68–82°F).

Check in: After 3–5 days you will notice cloudy or milky white patches forming on the surface of the scoby. This is a new baby scoby being formed. Once the new scoby is covering the liquid, take a clean teaspoon and taste the brew. This is where you'll get to know what you like – sweet or a little tart, both are fine, and it is up to you when you want to stop fermenting your tea. I like it best when the acidity is similar to that of a sweet orange juice, and it is slightly fizzy.

Strain and drink, or add flavours:
Reserve 250 ml (9 fl oz/1 cup) of your brew to start your next batch. You can now either strain the rest into a clean, airtight 1.5 litre (52 fl oz) bottle and store it in the fridge, where it will keep for up to 1 week, or you can add some extra flavourings and a second ferment stage to your fresh brew; see the instructions and flavour ideas on page 163.

KOMBUCHA TIPS

To take a break from brewing: Store your scobies in a kombucha hotel! This is a jar filled with scobies and kombucha tea from a previous batch, sealed with a lid and kept in the fridge. A scoby will keep well this way for 1–2 months.

Splitting a scoby: Once you have a living, breathing scoby in your possession, you can easily peel off a layer to give to a friend so they can join in the fun.

HOW TO USE

- Great as a base for cocktails … which turns the cocktail into a healthy drink, right?
- A perfect drink for the mid-afternoon slump.
- If you've let it ferment a little long and it errs on the side of sour instead of sweet, it is great in salad dressings in place of vinegar.

Once you've mastered the basic art of making Kombucha (see pages 158–161), you can have some fun and introduce some special flavour combinations to make your own unique brews. It's simple, really: add your chosen flavourings to a freshly strained batch of kombucha, leave it to ferment for an extra 2–4 days and enjoy. This extra fermentation stage will also make your kombucha even fizzier.

ORANGE & HONEY KOMBUCHA

MAKES: 1 x 1 litre (35 fl oz) bottle

METHOD

After straining your freshly made kombucha, add the honey and orange zest (or the other flavouring ingredients, if making one of the variations).

Pour your kombucha into a 1 litre (35 fl oz) plastic or swing-top bottle, leaving 5 cm (2 inches) of space at the top.

Seal the lid and store at room temperature for a further 2–4 days to allow carbon dioxide to develop. Make sure you keep an eye on the carbonation level, as you don't want the bottle to explode – this is very rare, but can happen! If you're nervous about potential explosions in glass bottles, use a clean plastic PET bottle the first few times, until you get the hang of it. Pressing onto the side of the plastic bottle will let you know how fizzy the drink has become – if it is firm to touch, the kombucha is very carbonated and you will need to drink it straight away.

When tasting the brew, carefully open the bottle over the sink, allowing the excess carbon dioxide to escape, and being wary of the pressure build-up.

When you are happy with the taste and level of carbonation, transfer your brew to the fridge, remembering to release the gas every day. This last process is crudely but appropriately called 'burping' and is essential, as the fridge will slow down the fermentation process, but will not stop the development of carbon dioxide. Use within a week or two.

INGREDIENTS

750 ml (26 fl oz/3 cups) strained, brewed Kombucha (page 161)
350 g (12 oz/1 cup) honey
2 tablespoons grated orange zest

VARIATIONS

GINGER & TURMERIC
875 ml (30 fl oz/3½ cups) strained, brewed Kombucha (page 161)
90 g (3¼ oz/¼ cup) honey
3 slices of fresh ginger
3 slices of fresh turmeric

ROOIBOS & VANILLA
625 ml (21½ fl oz/2½ cups) strained, brewed Kombucha (page 161)
250 ml (9 fl oz/1 cup) strong rooibos tea
55 g (2 oz/¼ cup) raw sugar
1 vanilla bean, split lengthways

KOMBUCHA & GUAVA
750 ml (26 fl oz/3 cups) strained, brewed Kombucha (page 161)
125 ml (4 fl oz/½ cup) guava juice

WATER KEFIR

I have no idea why we aren't all drinking water kefir every day. A naturally carbonated soft drink, it is slightly sweet and full of probiotics, so it is also very good for you. Not unlike kombucha, kefir is made using water kefir grains, which aren't real grains at all, but resemble clear jellybeans in the shape of cauliflower florets. Water kefir grains are in fact a type of scoby (a colony of beneficial yeasts and bacteria), which is what makes it probiotic as well as carbonated. You can buy kefir grains online and at good health food shops.

This recipe explains how to make your basic Water kefir, which takes 2–3 days and will give you a slightly carbonated drink. If you'd like to jazz it up by experimenting with different flavour additions, see page 169.

MAKES: 1 x 1 litre (35 fl oz) bottle

INGREDIENTS

55 g (2 oz/¼ cup) raw sugar
250 ml (9 fl oz/1 cup) hot filtered water,
     plus an extra 750 ml (26 fl oz/3 cups)
     filtered water
2 cm (¾ inch) knob of fresh ginger, sliced
1 thick slice of lemon
6 sultanas (golden raisins), 1 fig,
     or a few raisins
50 g (1¾ oz/¼ cup) water kefir grains

EQUIPMENT

2 x 2 litre (64 oz) glass jars and lids
small fine-mesh sieve
1 x 1 litre (35 fl oz) bottle, for storing
     the strained water kefir
small jar, for storing your water kefir
     grains for your next batch

From left to right: Water kefir; Passion pop
water kefir (page 169); Strawberry fizz (page 169).

WATER KEFIR METHOD

(1) **Prepare your jar:** Wash a 2 litre (64 oz) jar in very hot soapy water, then rinse well and air dry.

Make the sugar water: Dissolve the sugar in the 250 ml (9 fl oz/1 cup) hot filtered water and leave to cool.

(2)

Fill the jar: Add the sugar water to the jar, along with the remaining 750 ml (26 fl oz/3 cups) filtered water, the ginger, lemon, fruit and water kefir grains.

Seal and leave: Seal the lid so it is airtight. Leave the jar on the work bench at room temperature for 2–3 days, out of direct sunlight, where the temperature will stay between 20–26°C (68–79°F).

Check in daily: During those first 2–3 days, remove the lid each day and have a taste. You'll notice the liquid becoming less and less sweet. When it is barely sweet, it is time to strain it. The amount of time it takes to get to this point will vary depending on the temperature in your kitchen.

 《 (3)

Strain: Set a fine-mesh sieve over your other 2 litre (64 oz) jar. Strain the water kefir into it, reserving the jelly-like grains.

Store the reserved kefir grains: Store your reserved kefir grains in a small jar, with about 125 ml (4 fl oz/½ cup) of the strained water kefir, to start your next batch.

To drink now: Pour the strained water kefir into a clean 1 litre (35 fl oz) swing-top bottle. Store it in the fridge and use within 1 week.

To add further flavours: You can also flavour your kefir by adding a second ferment stage (see page 169). Keep your strained water kefir in the new 2 litre (64 oz) jar and proceed with one of the recipe variations on page 167, adding your chosen flavourings.

 (4) **To make the next batch:** Repeat the process outlined in steps 1 to 3, using 50 g (1¾ oz/¼ cup) of the reserved kefir grains from step 3 above, and 125 ml (4 fl oz/½ cup) of the strained water kefir as a starter culture.

To take a short break: Store the kefir grains in water in an airtight glass jar in the fridge; they will keep for up to 3 weeks.

For a long break: Find a friend to take care of your kefir grains, or dehydrate 50 g (1¾ oz/¼ cup) of the grains at a temperature below 42°C (108°F). Once the kefir grains are fully dry, store them in a snap-lock bag in the fridge, where they will keep for up to 6 months. To rehydrate, simply use 2 tablespoons of the dried granules to make your next batch.

HOW TO USE

- Use as a base for fruity cocktails in summer.
- Freeze in ice-block or popsicle containers for a healthy summer treat.
- Serve in small amounts to children as an alternative to sugary soda.

Passion pop water kefir (left),
Strawberry fizz (right).

Once you've made your batch of Water kefir (see pages 164–167), you can flavour it with juices and herbs, if you so desire. It'll only take an extra 6–12 hours, depending on the weather and how warm your kitchen is. When I added passionfruit and orange juice to my very first batch of water kefir, it catapulted me straight back to my childhood and my obsession with Passiona. I've been hooked ever since, and water kefir is now a regular brew in my kitchen.

PASSION POP WATER KEFIR

MAKES: 1 x 1 litre (35 fl oz) bottle

METHOD

Pour your strained, freshly brewed water kefir into a clean 2 litre (64 oz) jar. Add the passionfruit pulp, orange peel and orange juice (or the other flavouring ingredients, if making one of the variations). Give it all a good stir using a wooden or metal spoon.

Using a funnel, pour the mixture into a 1 litre (35 fl oz) swing-top or plastic bottle, leaving 5 cm (2 inches) of space at the top. Clean the rim with paper towel and close the lid.

Now leave the sealed bottle at room temperature for 6–12 hours to allow carbon dioxide to develop. Keep an eye on the level of carbonation, as you don't want the bottle to explode – this is very rare, but can happen! To be on the safe side, you can use a clean plastic PET bottle the first few times, until you get the hang of it. Pressing onto the side of the plastic bottle will let you know how fizzy the drink has become – if it is firm to touch, the kefir is very carbonated and should be consumed straight away; if it gives quite a bit, you can leave it for a few more hours.

When ready to taste, carefully open the bottle over the sink, allowing the excess carbon dioxide to escape, and being wary of the pressure build-up.

When you are happy with the taste and level of carbonation, transfer to the fridge, remembering to release the gas every day. This last process is called 'burping' and is essential, as carbon dioxide will keep developing in the bottle, even in the fridge.

Use within a week or two.

INGREDIENTS

750 ml (26 fl oz/3 cups) strained, brewed Water kefir (page 167)
60 g (2¼ oz/¼ cup) passionfruit pulp
1 strip of orange peel
60 ml (2 fl oz/¼ cup) orange juice

VARIATIONS

SHIRAZ GRAPE JUICE SODA
500 ml (17 fl oz/2 cups) strained, brewed Water kefir (page 167)
250 ml (9 fl oz/1 cup) water
125 ml (4 fl oz/½ cup) shiraz grape juice

SWEET SPICED COCONUT BUBBLES
750 ml (26 fl oz/3 cups) strained, brewed Water kefir (page 167)
60 ml (2 fl oz/¼ cup) fresh coconut water
1 star anise

STRAWBERRY FIZZ
750 ml (26 fl oz/3 cups) strained, brewed Water kefir (page 167)
60 g (2¼ oz/¼ cup) crushed fresh strawberries
1 cinnamon stick

VINEGAR

A few years ago, a very special friend of mine, Sam Hughes, gave me a flagon of honey-coloured semillon he'd made. When I pulled it out of the cellar a year later, I was heartbroken to see that the wine's seal was broken. It was drinkable, but not great. Unable to throw it away, I decanted it into a large jar and added the mother culture from some apple cider vinegar. Six months later I tasted it. To my surprise and relief, I found that my science experiment had yielded a truly exceptional vinegar. This is what I love about learning to cook from scratch. It isn't always about planning, hard work and mountains of ingredients – sometimes you have a crack at a project on a whim and end up with something really special.

To make vinegar, you just need good-quality booze and some unpasteurised vinegar or a vinegar 'mother' from a health food shop, and you're on your way.

MAKES: 2 x 750 ml (26 fl oz) bottles

INGREDIENTS

2 x 750 ml (26 fl oz) bottles of organic preservative-free wine, cider or sparkling wine
125 ml (4 fl oz/½ cup) unpasteurised apple cider vinegar (available from health food shops), or a vinegar 'mother' culture

EQUIPMENT

1 x 2 litre (64 oz) jar or ceramic crock funnel
clean tightly woven cloth, for covering the jar
rubber band or kitchen string, for securing the cloth
2 x 750 ml (26 fl oz) narrow-necked bottles with lids

VINEGAR METHOD

 Prepare your jar: Wash the jar or ceramic crock in hot soapy water, then rinse well and air dry.

 Fill your jar: Pour the wine into the jar, then add the vinegar or mother.

 Seal and leave: Loosely cover the rim of the jar with a tightly woven cloth, then secure with a rubber band or kitchen string. Leave the jar in a cool, dark, well-ventilated place.

 Check in: After a few weeks, start tasting and smelling your brew. Depending on the ambient temperature, the vinegar mother and the alcohol, fermentation can take anywhere from 3 weeks to 6 months, so just keep tasting until you like it and the alcohol has been transformed into vinegar.

 Decant and store: Decant your brew into smaller bottles, then seal and store in the pantry, where your vinegar will keep indefinitely. If you are concerned about oxidisation, you can process the sealed bottles in a saucepan of boiling water at 60°C (140°F) for 10 minutes.

HOW TO USE

- A must in any salad dressing with olive oil, mustard, salt and pepper.
- Use in any of your pickling recipes, such as Quick cucumber pickles (page 76) or Farmers' market pickles (page 71).
- Use in your Strawberry shrub (page 207).

CHAPTER SIX

WEEKEND PROJECTS

PASSATA

I was taught how to bottle puréed tomatoes by two lovely friends, Jessica and Laura, who are absolute pros and make it all look really easy. That's because it is. The catch is you need to be organised and not attempt it alone – I tried that one year with a toddler underfoot and nearly had a nervous breakdown. So, get yourself organised, invite a bunch of mates over, and have a crack at it with plenty of food and booze on hand to smooth the way.

Passata is best made with San Marzano or Roma (plum) tomatoes as these have a lower water content than other varieties and cook down to a beautiful sweet mess. You can order them from your greengrocer from mid summer.

I sterilise my jars using a sterilising solution from a home-brewing shop, but you could also sterilise them as you would jars for jam (see page 55). You'll also need a huge saucepan or stockpot to boil all the filled bottles or jars in (they need to be fully submerged), or you can use several smaller pans and pasteurise the bottles in batches.

MAKES: 10–12 x 750 ml (26 fl oz) bottles

INGREDIENTS

10 kg (22 lb) vine-ripened San Marzano or Roma (plum) tomatoes; each 1 kg (2 lb 4 oz) tomatoes should yield about one 750 ml (26 fl oz) bottle or jar of passata
sea salt

EQUIPMENT

large saucepan for blanching tomatoes
slotted spoon or scoop
large bowl, lined with a tea towel; or alternatively you can use a colander
a second large bowl
passata machine (known in Italian as a passapomodoro) or food mill funnel
funnel and ladle
10–12 sterilised brown or green 750 ml (26 fl oz/3 cup) bottles, plus metal bottle caps and capping machine (or you can use ordinary mason jars or bottles with sterilised sealable lids)
very large pan or stockpot to pasteurise the bottled tomatoes in; check all the bottles will fit inside, standing up or lying down flat
tea towel

PASSATA METHOD

Prepare the tomatoes: Wash the tomatoes to remove any dirt. Bring a large saucepan of water to the boil, then add about 10 tomatoes and leave for 1 minute, or until the skins blister slightly. Using a slotted spoon or scoop, transfer to a bowl lined with a tea towel to soak up any excess water, or place in a colander over the sink.

Squeeze out the juice: Over another large bowl, squeeze the cooled tomatoes with your hands. You want to break them up and release the seeds and juice, but keep the flesh and skins.

2 »

Process the tomatoes: Put the squeezed tomatoes into your passata machine or food mill and crank the handle. The puréed tomatoes will come out one side, the seeds and skins the other. Put the skins and seeds back through the machine to extract as much of the good stuff as possible, then discard.

Repeat with remaining tomatoes: Repeat steps 1–3 with another batch of tomatoes until you are finished; after a few batches, you'll need to pour the passata into a larger bowl or saucepan, ready to be decanted into the bottles.

Add salt: Add a good pinch of salt to the puréed tomatoes (or to taste).

Bottle: Using a funnel, ladle the passata into sterilised brown or green bottles, leaving about 3 cm (1¼ inches) at the top of each. Wipe the rims clean with paper towel.

(3) »

« (4)

Cap: Put a metal cap on the bottle and push down to seal, using a capping machine. If you are using jars, pour the passata into the jars, leaving 1 cm (½ inch) at the top of each. Tap gently to make sure there are no air bubbles, wipe the rims clean of wayward tomato juice and screw the lids on.

(5) »

Pasteurise the bottles: This next step is important to pasteurise the passata, which makes it 'shelf stable' for up to 1 year. Grab a very large saucepan or stockpot, making sure it is tall enough to hold the passata bottles standing upright and for them to be covered by water (including the lids); you could also lay the bottles flat, in layers. Place a tea towel in the bottom of the pan, to stop the bottles breaking as they jostle around in the boiling water. Carefully fill with the passata bottles. If you are nervous that they may rattle against each other and break, you can put each bottle in a sock before gently lowering them in. Fill the pan with cold water and bring to the boil; this can take a few hours. Reduce the heat to low and simmer gently for 30 minutes. Leave in the pan to cool to room temperature – this takes ages, so I just leave them overnight. Remove the bottles from the pan. Dry, label and store in a cool dark place for up to 1 year. Once opened, store in the fridge and use within 1 week.

Many a good sauce has been ruined by the hasty addition of tinned tomatoes, resulting in bitter garlic and crunchy onion. The key to a good tomato-based pasta sauce is to cook the onion very gently for a lot longer than you'd expect; it will become sweet and soft and form the basis for the perfect simple sauce.

Jazz this sauce up with anchovies, capers and chilli, or keep it simple and top with handfuls of sweet summer basil.

SIMPLE TOMATO SAUCE

MAKES: 500 ml (17 fl oz/2 cups)

INGREDIENTS

½ onion
4 garlic cloves
1 tablespoon olive oil
750 ml (26 fl oz/3 cups) Passata
    (page 177)
a big pinch of sea salt
a handful of basil leaves

METHOD

Peel and finely dice the onion. Peel and roughly chop the garlic.

Place a frying pan over low heat. Add the olive oil, then fry the onion for 10 minutes. Now add the garlic and continue frying for another 5 minutes, or until the onion is soft. Never rush this step, as the longer cooking sweetens and softens the onion, which is the foundation for your sauce; it should be lightly golden and translucent.

Pour in the passata, stir in the salt and turn up the heat for about 5 minutes, stirring now and then. When the sauce is the consistency you like, throw in the basil leaves, then turn off the heat.

Serve with your favourite pasta, with generous shavings of good parmesan cheese.

CORN TORTILLAS

This is an excellent project to try with a bunch of friends. Freshly cooked tortillas take only a few minutes to make, and taste intensely of corn, a little smoky from the dry-frying, and really fresh. Fill with one of the fillings suggested at the end of the recipe, or on page 186, then crack open a beer and stand back and admire your handiwork.

Tortillas freeze really well, so make a big batch and store some in the freezer; when you need them, simply reheat them in a dry hot pan with a sprinkling of water added.

You'll need a special flour called masa harina to make proper tortillas (don't try it with polenta because it won't work). Masa harina is made from corn that has been treated with lime via a process called nixtamalisation, which makes it easier to digest and more nutritious. You can find it at specialty food stores.

MAKES: 20

INGREDIENTS

500 g (1 lb 2 oz) masa harina
1 teaspoon sea salt
500 ml (17 fl oz/2 cups) water
1 tablespoon olive oil

EQUIPMENT

large mixing bowl
fork or wooden spoon
tea towels
tortilla press or a rolling pin
baking paper
small frying pan

TORTILLA METHOD

« **(1)** **Combine dry ingredients:** Pour the masa harina and salt into a large bowl and stir until well combined.

Add water: Add the water and oil, then mix to combine, using a fork or wooden spoon. Once the mixture is shaggy and still a little wet, tip it onto a floured work bench.

(2) **»**

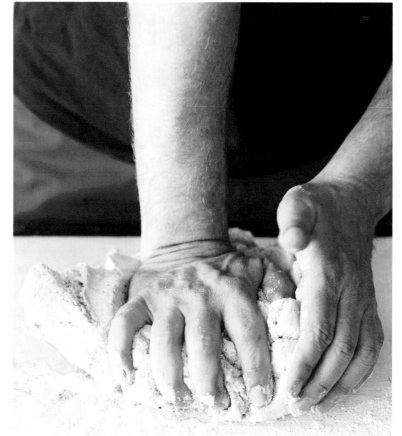

Knead: Quickly knead until the mixture comes together in a ball and is the consistency of soft playdough. If it is a little sticky, just add a pinch more masa harina. To test if you have the right amount of water, make a walnut-sized ball of dough and gently squeeze it. If it cracks, you need a touch more water. If it doesn't, you're right on track.

« **(3)** **Leave to rest:** Cover with a damp tea towel and leave to relax for 15 minutes, or a few hours if making ahead.

④ »

Roll into balls and flatten: Moisten your hands and divide your dough into 20 evenly sized balls. If you are using a tortilla press, place a ball of dough between two sheets of baking paper, place in the tortilla press and gently press to squeeze shut. If you don't have a press, flatten the ball into a disc, place between two sheets of baking paper and roll into a round about 5 mm (¼ inch) thick; take care to make them as thin as you can, otherwise they will be tough.

« ⑤

Fry: Heat a small frying pan until hot; you won't need any oil. Flip the tortilla off the baking paper onto your hand, then into the pan, and fry for about 30 seconds per side. Don't be tempted to move the tortilla as soon as you put it into the pan, as it will stick a bit at first.

Keep warm and eat: Stack your tortillas under a dry tea towel to keep them warm until you are finished.

HOW TO USE

- Place some shredded cheddar cheese and thinly sliced chorizo between two tortillas, then fry in a dry hot pan for an amazing toastie.
- Cut leftover tortillas into eights and fry in very hot oil to make traditional tortilla chips for nachos; you could also bake them until crisp.
- Wrap your tortillas around tasty fillings like crumbled chorizo sausage, thinly sliced steak, smoked chicken, grilled white fish or pulled pork; add some shredded cabbage, radish, coriander (cilantro), a crumbling of sharp white cheese and a big fat squeeze of lime juice.

Once you've made your Corn tortillas on page 183, here are some suggestions for different fillings for each season. Try to use whatever ingredients are plentiful and tastiest, such as mushrooms in autumn, and avocado in summer – and take care not to overstuff your tortillas, or they'll fall apart. Serve with your favourite fresh tomato salsa or hot sauce.

SEASONAL TORTILLAS

MAKES: each variation fills 4 tortillas

SPRING

200 g (7 oz) shredded barbecued chicken
1 large avocado, sliced
100 g (3½ oz) white cheese, such as
    queso fresco or feta, crumbled
Fermented chilli sauce (page 153),
    for drizzling
10 coriander (cilantro) sprigs
4 radishes, thinly sliced
lime wedges, to serve

SUMMER

4 white fish fillets (such as whiting), grilled
¼ small green cabbage, very finely shredded
¼ red onion, finely shredded
1 avocado, sliced
4 radishes, thinly sliced
crème fraîche or sour cream, mixed with
    a squeeze of lime juice and a sprinkling
    of sea salt, for drizzling
lime wedges, to serve

AUTUMN

2 large pine or field mushrooms,
    grilled or baked, then thinly sliced
finely shredded English spinach, or other
    seasonal greens
10 coriander (cilantro) sprigs
Fermented chilli sauce (page 153),
    for drizzling
100 g (3½ oz) sharp white cheese,
    such as queso fresco or feta, crumbled

WINTER

400 g (14 oz) pulled pork
1 red onion, sliced thinly and marinated
    in lime juice with a pinch of sea salt
    for 30 minutes, then drained
10 coriander (cilantro) sprigs
Fermented chilli sauce (page 153),
    for drizzling
lime wedges, to serve

WOK-SMOKED CHICKEN

Who doesn't love smoked meats? They're all the rage, but they're expensive to buy and store-bought versions often include unexpected nasties. It's not that hard to smoke your own meat and vegetables at home, and there's no need for fancy equipment and hours of your time. The easiest and most satisfying way is to grab your wok, foil and some tea, sugar and rice and get into it. Experiment with different meats and vegetables and vary the smoking mix according to what works best with each meat; just be careful not to add too much tea as this can make it bitter. For chicken you could add star anise and coriander seeds, or for duck, strips of orange peel and a cinnamon stick. Fennel seeds pair well with fish, and cumin seeds with eggplant (aubergine), or try fresh ginger, cloves and Chinese five-spice with pork.

If you want to make sure your fish or meat is really tender, I recommend brining it for an hour prior to smoking. To give an extra whack of deliciousness to chicken, duck and fish, you can also throw them on the barbecue or under the grill, or glaze them with honey and soy sauce after you have smoked them.

MAKES: 6 smoked chicken thighs

INGREDIENTS

6 chicken thighs, with or without
    bones and skin
50 g (1¾ oz/scant ⅔ cup) tea leaves
50 g (1¾ oz/¼ cup, lightly packed)
    brown sugar
150 g (5½ oz/¾ cup) uncooked
    jasmine rice

BRINE
1 litre (35 fl oz/4 cups) water
4 tablespoons fine sea salt
2 tablespoons brown sugar

EQUIPMENT

small saucepan
medium bowl
large wok with lid; if your wok doesn't
    have a lid, you can improvise with foil
    or the lid of a large saucepan
foil
small bowl
round wire cooling rack that fits inside
    your wok
tongs

WOK-SMOKING METHOD

« (**1**)

Make the brine: Heat 250 ml (9 fl oz/1 cup) of the water in a small saucepan. Stir in the salt and sugar until dissolved, then add the remaining water and leave to cool. Place the chicken in a medium bowl and cover with the brine. Leave in the fridge for 1 hour, then drain and pat dry. Place the chicken on a plate, cover and return to the fridge to dry out for a further 1 hour.

(**2**) »

Set up your wok: Line your wok with foil, making sure that it overhangs by about 10 cm (4 inches) all the way around.

Add your smoking mix: Combine the tea leaves, sugar and rice in a small bowl, then sprinkle over the bottom of your foil-lined wok. (If you placed this mixture directly in the wok, you'd end up with a burnt mess that would ruin it forever.)

« (**3**)

Make a drip tray: Using another piece of foil, crimp the edges to make an improvised round drip tray. Put the foil tray over the smoking mix in the wok, then place the wire rack inside the wok.

Start smoking: Put the lid on and heat the wok over high heat until you see wisps of smoke. Lower the heat and open the lid. Quickly put the chicken in and replace the lid.

(4) »

Seal the wok: If your wok doesn't have its own lid, crimp the foil edges over to seal the wok.

« **(5)**

Cook then leave: Cook over medium heat for about 20 minutes. Turn off the heat and leave for a further 20 minutes to infuse. Transfer to the fridge and leave for a few hours to cool. Slice and then serve!

HOW TO USE

- Smoke duck breasts for 20 minutes and glaze with plum sauce spiked with star anise. Serve in a winter salad with plums, radicchio leaves and chopped hazelnuts.
- For addictively sweet, sticky wings, smoke chicken wings for 20 minutes, brush with a marinade of soy sauce, honey, rice wine vinegar, ginger and garlic, then bake in a moderate oven for 10–15 minutes or until the dressing is nice and sticky.
- Smoke eggplants (aubergines) and a bulb of garlic for 30 minutes; peel and mix with tahini, yoghurt and lemon juice for a delicous take on baba ghanoush.
- Smoke fish such as trout for 15 minutes; serve with creamy scrambled eggs for an amazing breakfast.

I love this recipe because once you have the chicken smoked and glazed, which you can do the day before, this dish is on the table in less than 10 minutes. Serve with a bowl of seasonal salad greens or steamed new-season asparagus and snow peas (mangetout) drizzled with sesame oil and lemon juice.

SMOKED CHICKEN SOBA NOODLE SALAD

SERVES 4

INGREDIENTS

300 g (10½ oz) packet of buckwheat
   soba noodles
6 smoked chicken thighs (page 189)
1 bunch coriander (cilantro), stems and
   leaves chopped
1 chopped red chilli, to serve (optional)
lime cheeks, to serve

DRESSING
2 tablespoons tamari
1 tablespoon chilli sauce
1 teaspoon sesame oil
1 teaspoon grated fresh ginger

GLAZE
125 ml (4 fl oz/½ cup) tamari
   or salt-reduced soy sauce
125 ml (4 fl oz/½ cup) honey
   or maple syrup
1 tablespoon chilli sauce,
   such as sriracha

METHOD

Prepare the noodles according to the packet instructions. Combine the dressing ingredients in a small bowl, then drain the noodles and toss with the dressing.

Meanwhile, preheat the grill (broiler) to medium–high. Combine the glaze ingredients in a small bowl. Using a pastry brush, work the glaze over the chicken thighs, leaving a small amount of glaze to brush over the chicken halfway through cooking.

Place the chicken on the grill tray and cook for 1 minute, then reapply the glaze. Turn the chicken over and repeat, then thinly slice.

Divide the noodles among shallow serving bowls and arrange the chicken slices on top. Sprinkle with the coriander and the chilli, if using. Serve with lime cheeks for squeezing over.

GRAVLAX
HOME-CURED SALMON OR TROUT

The first time I ever caught a fish was also the first time I made gravlax. Beginner's luck saw me snag an 11 pound Chinook salmon off the coast of Oregon, and to this day I frequently feel the urge to brag about it. Needless to say, I've never caught another fish, and not from lack of trying.

When you have a fish that big to deal with, it is a good time to think about different preservation techniques. We had sashimi and some oven-roasted salmon that night, made gravlax to have in a few days time, and then cured the roe so we had beautiful pink caviar whenever we wanted it.

Gravlax is the Nordic name for salt-cured fish. The method suits salmon, but you can also use ocean trout or other oily, firm fish. This is a really impressive dish and absolutely dead easy. Preparing the salmon only takes a few minutes, but you need to leave it for a few days to cure, so start this project two days in advance.

MAKES: 800 g (1 lb 12 oz)

INGREDIENTS

2 tablespoons sea salt
140 g (5 oz/⅔ cup) granulated
    white sugar
2 bunches dill
zest of 1 lemon
800 g (1 lb 12 oz) very fresh salmon
    fillet, 4 cm (1½ inches) thick,
    with the skin on, and all the
    small bones removed

EQUIPMENT

small bowl
kitchen string
baking dish with sides
baking paper
weights, such as tins of tomatoes
    or small beer bottles
chopping board
very sharp knife

GRAVLAX METHOD

Assemble the cure and dish: Combine the salt and sugar in a small bowl. Lay three long bits of kitchen string over a baking dish, across the two long sides of the dish, spaced evenly apart. Drape a large piece of baking paper over the dish, making sure there is a generous overhang. Spread half the dill over the paper, then sprinkle with half the sugar and salt mixture, then half the lemon zest.

1 »

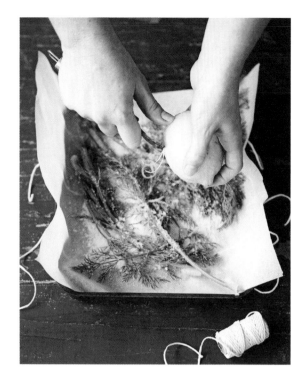

« **2** **Coat the fish:** Sit the salmon on top, skin side down. Evenly sprinkle the rest of the sugar and salt mixture over the salmon, then top with the remaining dill and lemon zest. The fish should be well covered.

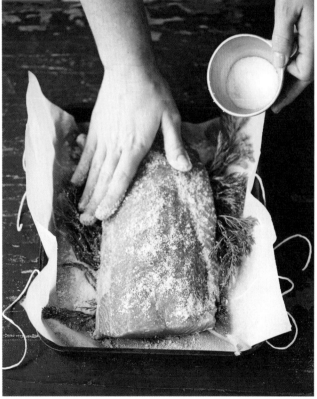

3 »

Wrap it tightly: Pull the edges of the baking paper over the fish and wrap it up like a present, tying with the strings.

Weigh it down: Grab two tins of tomatoes or small bottles of beer and place on top of the salmon. Weighing the fish down is not absolutely necessary, but will give a firmer gravlax that will be easier to slice.

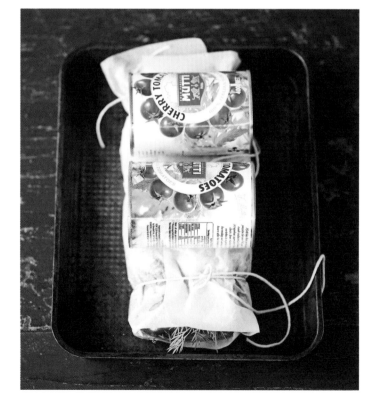

Cure in the fridge: Place in the fridge for 24 hours, turning once after 12 hours, and emptying the liquid that collects in the bottom of the dish.

Remove after 24–48 hours: When the fish feels firm to touch, take it out of the fridge. This recipe is not an exact science – the fish is safe to eat at any stage, so just remove when you think it is firm enough for you. This could be anywhere between 24 and 48 hours.

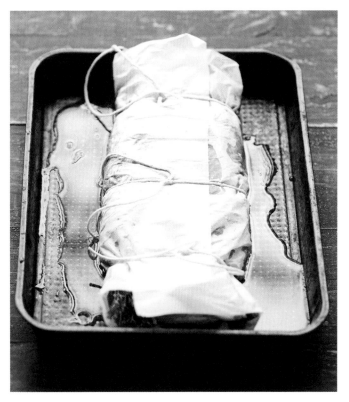

« 5

Get it ready to slice: Unwrap the fish. Remove the dill and lemon zest strips, then scrape off the curing mix. You can wash the salmon if you like, but it isn't necessary.

Slice and serve: Place the fish on a chopping board. Using a very sharp knife, slice it very thinly on the diagonal; the skin will help keep it in place as you slice. (If you're finding it hard to get thin slices, wrap the fish in foil and freeze for 10 minutes to firm up.) Once it has cured, the gravlax will keep for up to 3 days in the fridge.

HOW TO USE

- Load up a bagel with gravlax, Labne (page 98) or cream cheese, and a sprinkling of capers and dill.
- Grab some white bread, butter it liberally, and layer with gravlax. Remove the crusts and serve next to your cucumber sandwiches at high tea.
- Throw into an Asian-style salad full of fresh Thai basil, mint, coriander (cilantro), Vietnamese mint and a sprinkling of roasted peanuts.

This is the simplest, and I think the best, way to serve gravlax. To ensure you get lovely even slices, use your sharpest knife to carve the cured fish. If you are still finding it difficult, wrap the gravlax in foil and place it in the freezer for about 10 minutes to firm up slightly, which will make it easier to cut.

Grab a large serving board, a bottle of good dry white wine and a few friends and you'll have the afternoon sorted. If you don't have any marinated labne on hand, don't stress – just serve your gravlax with fresh Labne (page 98) or cream cheese instead.

GRAVLAX PARTY

SERVES 4

INGREDIENTS

400 g (14 oz) Gravlax (page 195)
1 jar of Marinated labne (page 103)
spicy greens such as radish leaves,
    sorrel or rocket (arugula)
home-made Crackers (page 133)
lemon wedges, to serve

METHOD

Thinly slice the gravlax, using a very sharp knife. Gently lay the slices on a sheet of baking paper.

Arrange the labne balls in a bowl and surround with a generous drizzle of the marinating oil.

Tear the greens into bite-sized pieces.

Arrange the gravlax, greens and crackers on a large serving board. Serve with the labne, and lemon wedges for squeezing over.

Great with a glass or two of chilled white wine.

SAUSAGES

Really good sausages are hard to come by. They should be juicy, full of flavour, and with just the right ratio of tender meat to good-tasting fat. The great news is that they are so easy to make, and you'll be beaming with pride when you serve your sausages made with your own signature spice mix. Add some home-made chutney and you are basically a god.

My favourite sausage is pork and fennel, with a hint of orange zest. I often just leave the sausage as one big coil, instead of making individual links, as I think it looks impressive – but mainly because I can't be bothered making the links. Play around with the spice mixes and different meats – venison, rabbit, chicken – along with the traditional pork and beef. You can hit up your local butcher to grind the meat for you, or if you have a grinder, just go for it. What you want is a medium grind, consisting of 20–30 per cent good-quality fat.

Take care to read the recipe carefully, as I've put in as many tips as I can to ensure you get the best result.

MAKES: 2 kg (4 lb 8 oz)

INGREDIENTS

1 tablespoon fennel seeds
1 tablespoon sea salt
1 tablespoon coarsely ground
   black pepper
finely grated zest of ½ orange
1.5 kg (3 lb 5 oz) minced (ground)
   pork shoulder
500 g (1 lb 2 oz) pork fat, minced
   (ground)

EQUIPMENT

small bowl
large bowl
meat grinder, if grinding the meat yourself
small frying pan
sausage stuffer – I prefer a small
   hand-cranked stuffer, but you can
   also use an electric one attached
   to a stand mixer
2 cm (¾ inch) natural casings; you can
   buy these from your butcher or online
pin
large airtight container
paper towel

SAUSAGES METHOD

Prepare the spice mix: Place the spices and orange zest in a small bowl and mix well.

Grind the meat: If you're grinding your own meat, spread the pork and pork fat on a tray and freeze for 15–20 minutes to get them really cold; meanwhile, chill the grinder parts in the fridge. (If you use warm utensils and meat, you'll lose some of the fat and end up with dry sausages!) Grind your meat and fat and place in a large bowl.

Season and knead: This is where you'll need to get a bit messy. Sprinkle the spices over the meat and fat and knead for about 3 minutes, until the mixture is sticky. This will ensure the spices are well incorporated; more importantly, it will develop the proteins in the meat and make for a better-textured sausage. (You can also use a stand mixer fitted with a paddle attachment if you are feeling lazy.)

Palm and pan test: The best way to check if you have kneaded the mixture enough is to take a small amount, form it into a patty and place on your palm. Now turn your hand over. If the mince doesn't fall off, it is ready. Take a small ball of the seasoned mince and gently fry it in a small frying pan for 3 minutes on each side. Let it rest for a minute, then check. It should have kept its shape and taste delicious.

《 ②

Clean the casings: Place your sausage casings under the tap and let the water run through them to make sure they are nice and clean, both inside and out, and don't have any holes.

Get your stuffer ready: Place the seasoned mince into the stuffer. Slip the casings onto the nozzle of your sausage stuffer, as though you are putting a stocking on a foot. (Feel free to make crude jokes at this point.) Leave a 10 cm (4 inch) tail at the end. The first thing that will come out of the stuffer is air, so don't tie the end yet.

Time to stuff: Slowly push the mince out into the casings. It will come out as a big coil. The sausage should be firm to touch, but your finger should still be able to leave a slight indent.

Make the links: When all the meat is in the casings and you have a beautiful big coil, you can either leave it like this – perfect for throwing on the barbecue as an impressive party dish! – or make individual links. If you want to make links, pinch the sausage at 10 cm (4 inch) intervals, twisting in alternate directions at each end. Tie off the end.

Check for air bubbles: Take a good look over the sausages. If you see any air bubbles, just prick these with a pin and smooth over. Place the sausages in a sealed container lined with baking paper or paper towel. Leave in the fridge for a few hours or overnight.

Cook: If they are not destined for the barbecue, I like to fry my sausages over high heat for 3 minutes, then finish them off in a hot oven for another 10 minutes. They are best cooked within 3 days.

HOW TO USE

- Add some breadcrumbs to your sausage mix and shape into burger patties.
- Combine the Pork & fennel sausage mixture (page 201) with chestnuts, torn bread, sage and butter, and use as a stuffing for chicken.
- Crumble your New York–style Italian sausage mixture (page 204) on pizzas with some tomato and fresh basil.

Here are four more of my favourite sausage recipes. I especially love the simple Kids' sausage, which is a hit in my household. Remember that all you really need is a good ratio of meat to fat (about 80/20), and then you can play around with all sorts of spices and herbs as flavourings. These recipes can also be used for making the hamburger patties for The best ever burger on page 86.

These sausages are made in exactly the same way as the ones flavoured with pork and fennel on page 201, so simply follow the instructions on pages 202–203, using the ingredients in your chosen version below.

CLASSIC SAUSAGES

MAKES: 2 kg (4 lb 8 oz)

BEEF SAUSAGES

1 tablespoon sea salt
1 tablespoon dried sage
2 teaspoons freshly ground black pepper
4 teaspoons dried thyme
2 teaspoons chilli flakes
2 kg (4 lb 8 oz) minced (ground) beef, containing about 30% fat

NEW YORK–STYLE ITALIAN SAUSAGES

2 teaspoons freshly ground black pepper
2 tablespoons sea salt
1 tablespoon fennel seeds
3 teaspoons cayenne pepper
2 tablespoons sweet paprika
1 tablespoon dried oregano
2 teaspoons chilli flakes
45 ml (1½ fl oz) red wine
2 kg (4 lb 8 oz) minced (ground) pork shoulder

SPICY LAMB SAUSAGES

2 teaspoons cumin seeds, toasted and ground
2 teaspoons coriander seeds, toasted and ground
2 teaspoons fennel seeds, toasted and ground
2 tablespoons sweet paprika
2 tablespoons sea salt
6 garlic cloves, crushed to a paste
1–1½ tablespoons harissa paste, depending on how spicy you like your sausages
2 tablespoons extra virgin olive oil
1.6 kg (3 lb 8 oz) lamb shoulder, minced (ground)
400 g (14 oz) pork fat, minced (ground)

KIDS' SAUSAGES

1 tablespoon sea salt
2 tablespoons finely chopped parsley
1.6 kg (3 lb 8 oz) minced (ground) beef
400 g (14 oz) pork fat, minced (ground)

STRAWBERRY SHRUB

A shrub is basically a vinegared fruit syrup. Sweet, tart and intensely refreshing, shrubs are enjoyed all around the world, and for good reason: they are delicious! You'll find them in Southern USA, where the name 'shrub' originated, all the way through to steamy South-East Asia, where they are spiked with sweet tropical fruits for instant relief from the humidity.

You can try different fruits in this shrub recipe – strawberries as I have here, or plums, peaches, pineapples and mangoes. Use whatever is in season and make sure the fruit is really ripe. I use regular white sugar in my shrubs; you could substitute with raw sugar, but don't venture further afield than that.

When you first make it, the vinegar can be a little dominant, so leave the shrub in the fridge for a few weeks and let the flavours balance out, or add a little more sugar if necessary.

Drink your shrub in a tall glass with lots of ice, soda water (club soda) and a jigger of gin.

MAKES: 1 x 800 ml (28 fl oz) bottle

INGREDIENTS

525 g (1 lb 2½ oz/3 cups) roughly chopped very ripe strawberries, stems removed
440 g (15½ oz/2 cups) granulated white sugar
500 ml (17 fl oz/2 cups) apple cider vinegar

EQUIPMENT

glass or ceramic bowl
another bowl, with a sieve set over it
wooden spoon
funnel
1 x 800 ml (28 fl oz) bottle and lid
ladle

STRAWBERRY SHRUB METHOD

(1) **Mix the fruit and sugar:** Put the strawberries in a glass or ceramic bowl. Pour the sugar over and leave for a few hours, or better still, overnight in the fridge. The sugar will slowly dissolve and draw out all the lovely juice in the berries. You'll end up with a bowl full of soft strawberries surrounded by sweet syrup.

(2) **Strain and squish:** Pour the mixture into a large sieve that is sitting over a bowl, to catch the syrup. Squish the berries with the back of a wooden spoon to extract as much juice as possible, then leave to strain for 30 minutes. Keep the sugared fruit pulp to serve over ice cream or Granola (page 12).

(3) **Add vinegar and bottle:** Stir the vinegar into the strained fruit syrup. It will have a very strong vinegar taste at this stage, which is normal.

(4) **Pour and store:** Fit a funnel into your bottle and ladle in the shrub. Seal and store in the fridge for a few weeks, after which the flavours will develop and the vinegar will mellow. You can of course drink it straight away, but you might want to add a little more sugar, as the vinegar will taste quite strong. It will keep in the fridge for up to 3 months.

(5) **Serve:** To serve, one-quarter fill a glass with the syrup, top with soda water and garnish as you please.

HOW TO USE

- Amazing as a base for summer cocktails. Use berry shrubs with gin or vodka; try citrus shrubs with bourbon or rum. Try a peach shrub with a dash of bourbon and topped with sparkling water.
- Instead of strawberries, use raspberries, rhubarb, peaches, blood oranges, mangoes, nectarines or even tangelos.
- Add different herbs and spices such as rosemary, Thai basil, ginger or mint.
- Use Champagne vinegar or red wine vinegar instead of cider vinegar – but avoid using balsamic or sherry vinegar as they are too strongly flavoured and expensive for this recipe.
- Try these seasonal flavour ideas. Spring: strawberry, Thai basil and peppercorns. Summer: Cherry, rhubarb and vanilla bean. Autumn: Plum and rosemary. Winter: orange and ginger.

INDEX

ACKNOWLEDGEMENTS

I had no idea how much work it would be to write a cookbook – especially with a baby on my hip. There are many people who helped make it happen and were so generous with their knowledge and time. I can't thank everyone enough who gave me the support and courage to turn this big idea into a book.

To Jill Dupleix and Terry Durack, who first approached me with the idea. I thought they were crazy! These heroes of the Australian food movement are two of the kindest and most supportive people I know. I cannot thank them enough for their confidence in me.

To the Murdoch team, hands down one of the best teams I have ever worked with. Full of good humour and serious talent – Hugh Ford, Katri Hilden and Virginia Birch. Massive thanks to Sue Hines for taking a punt on a new author. To Jane Morrow, my publisher and general all-round legend. I'm so grateful for her support, especially as I eased into the reality of being a working single mum.

To the shoot team: Cath Muscat, for her amazing photography and for making everything look so damn beautiful; Vivien Walsh (this lady has a way with a napkin!), thanks for such gorgeous styling; and Tracey Pattison, for knowing how to cook everything so well. A huge thanks to Jamie Madden for stepping in as our male hand model. He is a man of many talents.

Thanks to all my mates, without whose confidence in me this book would not have been written – Renee, Sally, Emma, Denis, Rocky, Nellie, Jasmine, Aaron, Berno, Imogen, Tom, Ange, Jess and Sherro. To my family – Moya & Allan, Patrick & Helen, Jim & Julie and Andy & Megan. A particular thanks to my brother Ben for helping with everything from washing-up to distracting a toddler to testing recipes. To Mac for his unwavering love and support. Thanks to Ginger for her ongoing inspiration and reminder that it takes a lot of hard work with a good dose of laughter to build the world you want to see. And to Sam Hughes for keeping it real from wherever you are. We miss you.

To the Real Food family: a huge thanks to my cooking mentors and friends of Real Food Projects. Particular mention needs to go to Matt Rothman, one of the best cooks and most generous teachers I know. I have learnt so much from him. To Jess and Laura, for teaching me the way of the passata and being willing models. To Anna Sokol for her milk kefir grains with a history. To Barbara Sweeney for her wordsmithing and constant encouragement. To Brendan Hilferty from Sparrow and Vine for boozing us up with his local Marrickville wines. To Rebecca Sullivan for her lovely Rosella Jam recipe and her inspiring work preserving our culinary heritage. To Jacquie Newling, the Colonial Gastronomer, for her frequent history lessons. And, finally, to Holly Davis and Jared Ingersoll for being so generous with their extensive knowledge and time. I'm lucky to count you all as friends.

Published in 2016 by Murdoch Books, an imprint of Allen & Unwin

Murdoch Books Australia
83 Alexander Street
Crows Nest NSW 2065
Phone: +61 (0) 2 8425 0100
Fax: +61 (0) 2 9906 2218
murdochbooks.com.au
info@murdochbooks.com.au

Murdoch Books UK
Erico House, 6th Floor
93–99 Upper Richmond Road
Putney, London SW15 2TG
Phone: +44 (0) 20 8785 5995
murdochbooks.co.uk
info@murdochbooks.co.uk

For Corporate Orders & Custom Publishing contact
Noel Hammond, National Business Development Manager, Murdoch Books Australia

Publishing Consultants: Jill Dupleix and Terry Durack
Publisher: Jane Morrow
Editorial Manager: Virginia Birch
Design: Hugh Ford
Editor: Katri Hilden
Photographer: Cath Muscat
Stylist: Vivien Walsh
Home Economist: Tracey Pattison
Production Manager: Mary Bjelobrk/Alexandra Gonzalez

A cataloguing-in-publication entry is available from the catalogue of the National Library
of Australia at nla.gov.au.

ISBN 978 1 74336 421 5 Australia
ISBN 978 1 74336 422 2 UK

A catalogue record for this book is available from the British Library.

Colour reproduction by Splitting Image Colour Studio Pty Ltd, Clayton, Victoria
Printed by 1010 Printing International Limited, China

The author and publishers would like to thank KitchenAid for providing equipment for the photoshoot.

IMPORTANT: Those who might be at risk from the effects of salmonella poisoning (the elderly, pregnant women, young children and those suffering from immune deficiency diseases) should consult their doctor with any concerns about eating raw eggs.

OVEN GUIDE: You may find cooking times vary depending on the oven you are using. For fan-forced ovens, as a general rule, set the oven temperature to 20°C (35°F) lower than indicated in the recipe.

MEASURES GUIDE: We have used 20 ml (4 teaspoon) tablespoon measures. If you are using a 15 ml (3 teaspoon) tablespoon add an extra teaspoon of the ingredient for each tablespoon specified.